LEAVES OF A......

A New Poetry Collection
1988–1998

Bernard Kennedy

Marmara Press

First published 1998.

Books containing works by the author:
"*Rainbows and Stone*" an anthology of modern Irish poetry, 1988.
"*Context Reality*" Vantage Press, 1988 (a first collection).
"*Poetry Now*" (1993) Peterborough, UK. Argosy; Mentor Publication, 1991.

© Bernard Kennedy.

All rights reserved. Except for the quotation of short passages for the purposes of criticism and review, no part of this book may be reproduced, stored in a retrieval system, or transmitted in any form without the written permission of the author.

© Photos through book by Bernard Kennedy.

With thanks to John Ennis for permission to quote from 'Arboretum'.

With acknowledgements to Fr. Michael Drennan, S.J., for permission to photograph Manresa Grounds; to Fr. Michael Bannon, Diocesan Secretary, St. Michael's, Longford, for permission to use photographs from the 'Latin School', Boylan/Gray, on Page 76; to Dúchas, The Heritage Centre, St. Stephen's Green, Dublin 2, for permission to photograph at Mellifont Abbey (pages 44, 46 and 104); and to Alice Hughes for permission to use the photographs on pages 8, 20 and 54.

And finally, my thanks to Matthew Folan and Paul Westlin of Gemini for their design input to the digital-printing of this book.

ISBN 0 9534802 0 8.

Printed by Gemini International Ltd
Herbert Street, Dublin 2, Ireland.

Published by Marmara Press
3 Sweetmount Drive, Dundrum, Dublin 14, Ireland.

To my mother and father (Alice Hughes and William Kennedy);
to family and friends; to Therese; and to Kudret Kimyaci (Istanbul).

"The sun itself needs our love, grey Dante wrote,
Where there is no vision, people peter out.
They harbour no thought of spring, or harvest."

Arboretum, J. Ennis

*"The poet is the thief of fire:
He is responsible for humanity, even animals,
His inventions can be smelt, felt, heard.
He brings forth form.
If it is formless, he brings forth formlessness.
The first romantics were seers:*

    *Donc le poete est
    Vraiment voleur de fue."*

Arthur Rimbaud, 1854-1891

"Where there are no visionaries,
People peter out"

JOHN ENNIS, ARBORETUM

"A poem is like a painting: The closer you stand to this one the more it will impress you, whereas you have to stand a good distance from that one: This one demands a rather dark corner, but that one needs to be seen in full light and will stand up to the keen-eyed scrutiny of the art CRITIC: this one only pleases you the first time you saw it, but that one will go on giving PLEASURE however often it is looked at".

HORACE: 65 BC – 8 BC
On the Art of Poetry.

Table of Contents

Marlay Park Sound	3
The Northern Man	4
Celtic Turks	5
Midas	7
The Walker	9
Sunny October Evening	11
Autumn Shades	13
Angel Guest	14
The Funeral Bell	15
Night	16
Bad News	18
Near the Gate of Heaven	21
Like a Ripe Fruit (to the Resurrection)	23
Balbriggan Evening	25
The Oyster of God	26
Gathering Chestnuts	27
Murder Machine	29
Lady of the Grotto	30
Christmas Light	31
Echo of the Night	32
St. Philomena's Crib	33
Bounding Dog	35
The Quarter Diamond	36
A T.V. Personality	37
Pearl Merryweather	38
Nun	39
Paradise Garden	41
Nature's Graces	43
Approaching Winter	45
Boatman from the River Styx	47
When Earth was Kissed by Mars	51
Marmara Dance	53
Pink Hydrangea Bloom	55
Laughter	57
Old Blue Eyes	59
Sloe Bush	61
The Cat and the Starling	63
Ataturk Soldier	65
Minerats and Mosques	67
From Trabzon to Gumushane	69
Bombed in Omagh	71

Dark Lover in the Sonnet	73
September Morn	74
Ortakoy	79
Yeni Kapi	81
Two Weeks of Rain	83
Happy Priest	86
Ani	89
Rubilev's Icon	91
The Crucifixion	92
Woodland Walk	93
Mise Éire	95
School	97
For Bayram	99
A Drive on Fatih Bridge	101
From Van in the Air	103
Autumn Benediction	105
Leaves of Autumn	107
Silence	108
The Giant Oak	109
Eternal Seeds	111
Introibo ad Altare Dei	112
After the Storm	113
Angel of Jabbok	114
Poor Father Shawn	115
Luther Dog	118
Throw-away Dog	119
Plants for the Autumn	121
Index of First Lines	123
Notes on the Poems	124

The following collection of poems was gathered from the period 1988 to 1998. Some were written in Balbriggan, Palmerstown and Dundrum, or Rathfarnham. Others were compiled in Istanbul, and each bears the atmosphere, in words, of that place. Poetry is the word alive, logos, encountered in the reader's own understanding.

Words are creative entities, which in turn can stimulate other words and thoughts. They are urged by beauty, and in turn encapsulate, and describe what is metaphysical. Poetry is a vocation of sorts, hearing the unspoken, and sensing the base core of existence, and thus its direction.

Poetry can be prayer, like the Psalter, containing, inspired reactions to the divine impulse. It is important not to categorise either the poet, or the poem, as each is a different hearing of the same experience, yet the antenna picks it up differently.

Poetry is a creative art, as architecture, painting, music, giving birth, love and the activity of inspiration. Some of the great poets like Lorca, Whitman, Hopkins, Kavanagh, Heaney, Brodsky, O'Shearcaigh, Boland, Ní Dhomnaill, are midwives to mystery, of different continents and times.

To enjoy poetry, is to be still and hear, and that, in itself, is to give birth in our inner being, to the release mystery demands. It is deeper than uninspired activity. In the words of the poet John Ennis, in a poem Arboretum, "without vision, things 'peter out' ". How apt for the Martha's doing without inspiration or vision, which is the house on sand. Poetry is of the visionary, of that order of things.

Bernard Kennedy,
September 1998.

HEEL, HEEL, AND CONSTANT PEAL

MARLAY[1] PARK SOUND

HEEL HEEL, AND CONSTANT PEAL
OF BELL, THREE THREES NINE.

HUSBANDS AND WIVES
LOVERS, PALS, PRAMS AND DOGS, AND
OLD RETIRED, AWAIT AND CATCH THE SOUNDS
OF PAST AND FUTURE.
OTHERS JOG AND FIT WALK, STRIDE A REGIME,
OF BENEDICTINE BODY FITNESS IN THIS,
OLD SITE, THAT DID ASPIRE THUS IN SPIRITUAL
KEN.

I LOVE THE SOUTH OF DUBLIN,
AIR AND VIEW AND, RAISED-EYES, TO HILLS,
THE ISSUES ARE REFINED AND NOT CONFINED,
BY THOUGHTS FROM
GORGE, VALLEY, NEST OR POOL. IN POLITICS,
VIEW IS FRESH AND SMART. AND RELIGION,
TALKS, OF GOD AND WOMEN PRIESTS AND MORALS
MOVE
FROM MOUNTAIN VIEW, NOT ECHO CONFINED
SHOUT.
THE ANGELUS BELL NOW STOPS TO RING AND
SOON,
THE EVENING WHITECHURCH BELL ANNOUNCES
EVEN SONG

PRAISE THE GOD OF CREATING, NOT CREATED
PAST,
BUT UP TO THE HILLS LIFT THINE EYES.

(Marlay 1988)

THE NORTHERN MAN[2]

THERE IS A LINE,
A BORDER LINE OF PERSONALITY MIND
THAT STARTS PAST SWORDS
AND TRAVELS NORTH
INCLUDING DONEGAL.

NORTH OF THAT LINE LIES DIFFERENT TYPES,
IN VIEW, AND HEART-FELT THOUGHT,
SOME LIVE REPUBLIC AND SOME
LIVE ON, BUT NEITHER DO BELONG,
FOR THE BORDER STARTS
JUST PAST THAT SPOT AND NO SOLUTION FOUND.
ITS TROUBLES ROAM THERE,
AND BETJEMAN FOUND THEM DOUR
CHURCHILL DREARY AND EVEN STILL THE NO, NO CALL,
IS FULL STOP IN THEIR MIND.

THERE IS A LINE A BORDER LINE
OF PERSONALITY KIND.
SO LET THEM MOVE THE BORDER THEN,
JUST AT THAT SPOT IN SWORDS,
AND ULSTER MEN AND ORANGE MEN
CAN MARCH THEN
UP AND DOWN,
AND OTHERS COME BELOW THAT LINE AND LIVE
IN GREEN AND PEACE,
WE WILL THEN BE A HAPPY LAND,
THE QUEEN CAN COME TO TEA.
FOR WE ARE USED TO QUEENS YOU SEE
WHO ALSO SIT FOR TEA,
CALL IT DUCHY CALL IT CAMP,
IT IS A WAY OF CARE.

FOR THERE IS A LINE A BORDER LINE
OF PERSONALITY KIND,
IT STARTS AT SWORDS AND TRAVELS NORTH,
INCLUDING DONEGAL.

(Balbriggan 1991)

STRAINING WRESTLERS, their muscles taut beneath the sheen of olive oil, search for each other's weakness during a contest in Edirne held annually for more than 600 years. Wrestling has always been the favourite Turkish sport. Turks perennially win in international competitions, and they can wrestle in almost any style. The tradition of oiling their bodies is an ancient one.

CELTIC[3] TURKS

EASTWARD SLAVE,
CELTIC SERVANT FROM GREEN LAND TO GYNTIANIA
SOLD AS WORKHORSE ON GALLEY SHIP
IN FOREIGN LAND
TO MIKLAGARD.

A DECORATED GLASS
WITH GOLD FROM ISTANBUL YET
JET OF IRELAND
MAKES TO COUSIN.

OISIN MIKLAGARD
IN TURKEY SWEET
SOUL COMES HOME.

(Istanbul 1988)

O BOLD DISCOVERY, HAPPY FAULT

Mosque in Edirne, Turkey.

MIDAS

CRACKING ROCK OF BURNING COAL,
WHOSE EXCAVATION'S HEAT,
REVEALS A HOT, MOLTEN, INTERIOR.
MIDAS LIKE LAZARUS,
STEPS FORTH FROM THE TOMB
IN ANATOLIAN PLATEAU.

A GORDION KING
THIS MIDAS MAN
A PHRYGIAN MONARCHY
BEFORE THE CHRIST.

O BOLD DISCOVERY; HAPPY FAULT
FOR IT IS NOT A TRACIAN MYTH
OF CYBELENE THOUGHT
BUT GOLDEN
RESURRECTION

(Istanbul 1988)

I MET MY FATHER,

William Kennedy (Pictured 1956).

THE WALKER

I MET MY FATHER, ON
THE HILL OF THE ROAD,
AT KILMASHOGUE'S.
HE WAS STRIDING DOWN FROM
HIS MOUNTAIN WALK
AND I ASCENDING.

HIS SUNDAY STROLL,
AND HE WAS FIT THEN,
"TAKE IT EASY, I WILL SEE YOU AT TEA".
I RECALL NOW, HIS OWN AGE,
THAT SAME TURN AND STRIDE,
SHOWING HIM INTO HIS BED
AND HIS RESTING PLACE.

ON THAT TURN AT KILMASHOGUE,
JUST THERE, AT THE MILL RUIN,
THE NEW COLUMBA'S GATE,
LIFE GOES FAST
AND GENERATIONS PASS,

"TAKE IT EASY
I'LL SEE YOU AT TEA".

(Rathfarnham 1995)

A DIVINE SHORE

Manresa, Dublin.

SUNNY OCTOBER EVENING

OVER TWENTY-THREE YEARS AGO AND SINCE,
I HAVE PRAYED AND SEARCHED
THE HOLY PATTERN OF LIFE,
THE CARTOON OF GOD'S FRESCO.

AT TWENTY-THREE AND NOW AT FORTY-THREE,
I HAVE LEFT THE WORLD TO SEE THE HAND
OF GOD AND BE HIS PEACE.
HIS CALM IN THE WARM OCTOBER,
HIS COLOUR, IN THE SILENT FLOWER OF
CONVERTED BARROWS, HANGING OFF THEIR
BORDER FLOWERS.
JUST THERE, AND BEING NICE.

THEY ALSO SERVE,
AN OASIS OF CAUGHT GRACE,
AND SEARCHED MAPS, FOR GODS
TOPOGRAPHY.

AND LISTING LIVES,
IN GRACE FILLED HARBOUR,
AT MANRESA[6],
A DIVINE SHORE.

(Manresa 1995)

GOD WALKS IN EVENINGS THERE

AUTUMN SHADES

I SAW A ROOK RUSH DOWNWARDS
LIKE A BLACK TARGETING BOMB;
AS IF THE RUSTY LEAF CURLED UP,
MOUSE-LIKE, WERE FOOD
FOR PREY.

A GARDENER'S SMOKING LEAVES, OF
AUTUMN,
AN ODOUR OF YEARS-END
HANGS ABOUT
IN BURNING LEAVES, AND
CHANGING COLOURS OF SUMMERS GONE.

RUSTY BROWNS AND REDS
AND WALLS.
ONCE DARKEST GREEN
NOW RED AND GOLD,
BUT WILL BE GREEN AGAIN.

THE GARDENS ARE THE SANCTUARIES
OF GOD'S THOUGHTS, GOD'S HUSHED
PARLOUR OF VISITORS CONVERSATIONS,
GOD WALKS IN EVENINGS THERE,
AND AMONG NATURE'S QUIET.

(Manresa 1995)

NOT ALWAYS IN A SWISH OF WINGS

ANGEL GUEST

GABRIEL COMES AND RAPHAEL TOO

WHEREVER YOU HAVE FELT
A LASTING LOVE AND JOY,
LOOK INTO THE GUEST AND SEE
THE ANGELS' TRACES.

NOT ALWAYS IN A SWISH OF WINGS
BUT MORE A CAUSE THAT
INVOKES AND SINGS
AND GUIDES TO DIVINEST PLACES.

TO KNOW THE SOUND
OF THESE SOFT BEINGS
EXCEPT WHEN NOW
SURPRISED WE SHOW
THIS LOVE TOWARDS HIM IS
LEANING.

(Manresa 1995)

OR A YOUNG, FULL OF PROMISE

THE FUNERAL BELL

IN THE DISTANCE?, OVER THE TOPS OF ROOFS,
TOLLS, SLOWLY, SADLY, THE FUNERAL BELL.
SOME CORPSE, IS BROUGHT THROUGH THE
DOOR OUT,
THE DOORS OF RESURRECTION.

I CAN ONLY HEAR THE SLOW, SAD TOLLING.
THE FUNERAL OF A CHARACTER,
BIG AND LARGE AND JOLLY OF LIFE.
OR A YOUNG, FULL OF PROMISE, SNATCHED
FROM A LIFE NOT LIVED.
MAYBE A VAGABOND, OR THIEF, OR
A SMALL CROWD,
A PRIEST, AND FRIENDLY GUARD.
BUT THROUGH THOSE DOORS, THOSE
BAPTISM AND WEDDING DOORS,
GOES ONE TO RESURRECTION
AND TO LIFE.

(Manresa 1988)

The 'heroic conception of the human will': Michelangelo's David

FOR NIGHT IS DARK AND ONLY SELF IS TRUE

NIGHT

I LOVE TO HEAR THE SILENCE OF THE NIGHT,
THAT TIME, WHEN DISTANCE DRAWS SO NEAR,
AND MEMORIES COME, AND FAR SOUNDS,
UNDISTURBED,
SO CLOSE.

FOR NIGHT IS DARK AND ONLY SELF IS TRUE,
A SELF WHOSE REST AND PAST, ARE
ONLY BREATHS AWAY.
YET FOR SOME,
THE NIGHT MAY HAUNT AND FEAR,
ITS CONSCIENCE TIME, WHEN CURTAINS
CLOSED ARE DRAWN,
SO TOO, ONES INNER SELF AND PAST,
TO JOY OR FRIGHT, THE
INNER SPIRITS WILL.

IT IS A BLESSED THING, THIS NIGHT,
WAS IT NOT NIGHT WHEN CHRIST CAME HOME,
AND BALANCED JUDAS EVIL DEED.
AND BLESSED NIGHT,
WHEN MONKS NOW RISE AND PRAY.
AND NICODEMUS,
FOR LACK OF SLEEP,
CAME HOME.
THE LADY OF THE NIGHT CAME TOO,
HER STUMBLING LED HER HOME.

IN THE DARKNESS OF THE WELL
THE MAGI SAW THE STAR IN DAY,
AND IN THE PSYCHE DWELLS OUR HEART.

O BLESSED NIGHT,
FOR ROLLING BACK THE STONE,
THE ANGELS LET IN LIGHT, AND FINISHED NIGHT.
NIGHT NO MORE.

THE SILENCE OF THE NIGHT IS DEEPLY RICH,
AND HOMEWARD BOUND, WE REST
AND SOUND OUR HOPE,
AND LASTING JOY
DWELLS HERE,
IN SHADOWS OF THE NIGHT.

(Palmerstown 1995)

HE WAS A BIG MAN

BAD NEWS

THE PRIEST JUST RANG TO SAY,
"BAD NEWS, TOMMY IS DEAD"
AND NOW, WITH A GLASS OF ALE
I SIT AND THINK
"TOMMY IS DEAD".
HE WAS A BIG MAN, A FATHER MAN,
A NEIGHBOUR AND HUSBAND MAN,
A CHILDLIKE MAN.

WHOSE SON IN YOUTH AND
LAUGHTER
AND CONFIDENCE, CANCER-CAUGHT,
DIED.

AND NOW TOMMY FOLLOWS HOME.

WHEN HE CRIED AT THE CHURCH, FOR
HIS SONS ENDED SMILE,
HE WAS BIG, WITH TEARS.
WHEN WITH HIS SON
GROWING UP, WAS WILD WITH LIFE,
HE WAS BIG IN UNDERSTANDING.
HE, WHO HAD THE EYE OF GIRLS,
AND MOVED THE PRIEST FURNITURE AFTER WORK,
AND CALLED TO SAY, "I'M ENGAGED",
AND THEN DIE.
HE WAS BIG WITH HOPE.
WHEN HE SAT IN THE HOSPICE,
AND PLAYED A TAPED SINATRA SONG,
INTO HIS SONS COMA,
AND HELD HIS WIFE AT THE GRAVE AND HER
SHOCKED HAND IN THE HOSPITAL
AND SAT IN THE PUB
TO TALK, AGAIN,
OVER A PINT
"HOW WAS IT ALL SO.
GOD MUST HAVE HIS WAYS".
HE WAS A BIG MAN.

LORD GIVE HIM A BIG WELCOME
BRING INTO VIEW, NOW O LORD,
WHAT YOU ALWAYS SAW.

(Palmerstown 1995)

Priory (opposite St Enda's), now demolished.

NEAR THE GATE OF HEAVEN

HAVE I GROWN ONWARDS SO FAST,
THAT NOW I DO NOT BLUSH,
AT THE STATUE OF A NAKED
MAN LOOKING THROUGH
THE PATH,
ON WHICH THE WAYFARER GOES ROUND
PAST PEARSE' DREAM.

PAST THE LAKE
WHERE SWAM TWO BIRDS,
THEIR TUTORS FREE,
FROM BLIND PURSUITS AS HE TAUGHT,
NEAR THE GATES OF HEAVEN,
NEAR THE POND OF INNOCENT SPLASH.

UNTIL THE SNAKE OF TERROR,
GAINED ITS HOLD AND STILL HOLDS SWAY
AND BITING THROUGH THE APPLE SKIN
UNLEASHED
A DRAGON FATE
THIS BEAUTY, THAT IS TERRIBLE,
THAT WILL PASS,
AND I GO SORROWFUL
BACK THROUGH THE GATES
TO THE WORLD.

(Rathfarnham 1988)

I SAW A SMALL GREEN SHOOT

LIKE A RIPE FRUIT (TO THE RESURRECTION)

A SMALL SEED IS A CHILD
TO WATER FEED AND NOURISH GROWTH.
ITS GREAT POTENTIAL WAKING UP
AND WEATHER STORMS, AND ADAPT A ROOT.

THEN A BLUSH OF STYLE AND CLASS,
GAINS ITS PLACE IN GROWING SEARCH,
AND LOVE ITS SWAYS RIGHT TO THE SHOOT,
IT'S BEAUTIFUL TO BEHOLD THE FRUIT.

AND SOON, AND VERY SOON,
THE ROSE WILL FADE, AND LEAF GO DRY,
BUT TALL AND STATELY,
BIRTHING LIFE AND ENERGY FEEL,
IT STANDS AND SOME.

FELLING IS A NASTY SWAY
ANDANTE HELL LIKE FIRE,
BUT YESTERDAY,
I SAW A SMALL GREEN SHOOT
BESIDE THE FALLEN LOG.

(Rathfarnham 1988)

AND A PROTESTANT SPIRE

BALBRIGGAN[10] EVENING

I THINK I LIKE THE EVENING BEST OF ALL,
THE SUMMER STICKY EVENING,
AS I TRUDGE UP CLONARD HILL
AND LOOK BACK AT THE SEA AND
ITS TOWN.
WHERE PIRATES WOULD LAND.

"NICE EVENING FATHER",
AND THROUGH HAGAN'S CROSS
WHERE FARMERS TALK OVER GATES,
ABOUT NEW POTATOES AND DUTCH TOMATOES,
KILLING THEIR PRICE.
THEN DOWN FLEMINGTOWN,
WHERE PLANES FROM THE CAMP,
DUCKS WEAVE, SILENT LIKE, A FILM
BLACK AND WHITE OF RESISTANCE.

THE OLD COTTAGE, THE LONGEST ONE,
WITH ITS THATCHED ROOF AND FOOTBALL
PLAYERS NEXT DOOR IN WHOLESOME FUN.
TO THE TOWN WITH TWO CHIMNEYS,
AND A PROTESTANT SPIRE
AND THE LADS BY THE INN,
THE OLD MEN AT THE COURTHOUSE
AND CRICKET BY THE PITCH.
THE EVENING IS A DIFFERING LIGHT.

(Balbriggan 1984)

THE OYSTER OF GOD

TROUBLED SOULS, WITH DISJOINTED LIFE,
AN AWARENESS
SO SLIDINGLY-SLOW, YET REAL,
OF GROWING, AGEING OLD.
A FAT, FAT, BARK FOR FREE, FELLING FIRE,
ONCE GREEN STICK FRESH SWISH,
 AND SUPPLE SWING,
EVEN THE GREEN-FINGERED FELLOW IS GONE.

RISING SAP, HANDSOME PALE LOVER,
CLIMBING, SCALING AND SINKING FINGERS,
EAGERING,
LIVES CREVICES,
CLIMBING.
AFTER THE PEAK,
THE CRUCIBLE OF THE ORDINARY.

AND GRACE IS CRUSHED IN ITS VALLEY,
OF INTERMINGLING SOUNDS,
WEATHER, SIGHTS, ROOTS OF GROWTH
AND SLUSHING WATERFALL,
JOY PAIN,
THE OYSTER OF GOD

(Manresa 1984)

WITH BROKEN BRANCH-BENT BROOM

GATHERING CHESTNUTS

NOW SEPTEMBER COMES AND SCHOOL BEGINS,
AND BOYS KNOCK CHESTNUTS DOWN,
WITH BROKEN BRANCH-BENT BROOM,
STRENGTHENED ON SHOULDER SAFE STRETCH.

HOW PLAYFULLY THE YOUNG CAN REACH,
A TROPHY SHARED, EACH FALLING LAUGH,
AND INNOCENCE, IT CANNOT CATCH
CAUTION,
CHESTNUT COILED CONKER,
FOOLISH FUN.

THIS IS YOUTH IN AUTUMN MEADOW
CARELESS, CAREFREE, LITHE, LUSTFUL,
SEPTEMBER STEALS OUR JOY,
AND I ROMANTIC MIND REMEMBER.

(Balbriggan 1992)

BUT AFTER SCHOOL THE JOY AND RUN

MURDER MACHINE

NOW SCHOOL BEGINS AGAIN,
AND STUDENTS HEAR THE THUD,
AND THUMP TERRIBLE,
OF TEACHERS BOOKS ON DESK
AND YOUNG MAN'S BRAIN.

THE NEAT ORDERED CLASS GO HIGH,
TO BEST-BREAST HIGH,
AND PROUD OF SEDUCTION CERT
OF ADULT SCHEMES OF WORK,
AND SCHEMING BUSINESS PLAN.

THE LIVING HEART GROWS COLD
HARD IN DREARY SCHOOL PARADE GROUND
STAND, SIT, INSPECTOR, SIR, PASS, GRADE.
BUT AFTER SCHOOL THE JOY AND RUN,
AND LAUGH, OF PASSING OUT,
AND ALL ACHIEVE THE SAME IN LIFE.
YET HAPPIER THE SCOUNDREL,
WHO DUCKS AND DIVES,
AND INWARDLY LAUGHS LONG.

(Balbriggan 1992)

LADY OF THE GROTTO[11]

MOTHER, OUR HUMAN GODS RELATIVE,
BETROTHED TO CROSS, CROWN, CALVARY,
AND SINGER OF OUR PENTECOST BIRTH,
EXULTED LIFE, NUNC DIMITTUS
OF CHRIST AND CREATION,
COSMOS CREATIVE.

COMPLETE, YOUR STAND OF PRAYER,
THE CHILD, THE YOUNG AND SAYER
OF PRAYERS, HEARD AND SENT.
THE COMPLETED CROWN OF REWARD,
MOTHER, MATER,
BE BETROTHED TO US TOO.

(Balbriggan 1992)

CHRISTMAS LIGHT

AT THE DARKEST, DEADEST, DEPRESSED
NATURE'S HOUR,
HOLINESS YEASTED A LIGHT.
A GLIMMER, SLOWLY SEEN,
AND THEN HOPE BURNED.
AND KNOWING SLOWLY CAUGHT.

THIS IS CHRISTMAS, LIGHT AND DARK,
AND DARKNESS DIMS,
AND NATURES CANVAS,
PAINTS THE INNER MEANING.
BORN IN A CAVE,
THE FIRST ETCH OF REDEMPTION.

(Balbriggan 1992)

ECHO OF THE NIGHT

THE SILENT NIGHT MAKES LOUD THE HISSING LOG,
THE DISTANT LORRY CHANGING UP AND DOWN ITS GEAR,
AND SMALL HOUSE LIGHTS, ARE BIG AND WARM IN FOG,
TO GUIDE THE TRAVELLER HOME TO LOVE AND CHEER.

FOR SOME THE NIGHT IS DARK, FOR SOME SOULS, BRIGHT.
TO REST OF BODY AND GIVE THE MIND A SPACE,
WHERE HEARTS WILL DREAM OF LEISURE'S DISTANT LIGHTS,
AND OTHERS, YET IN HOURS, WILL GAZE GOD'S FACE.

SPRINKLE STARDUST, SANDMAN, NOW, SO I CAN SLEEP,
AND IN THOSE DREAMS, WHERE I DO LONG TO GREET,
MY FRIENDS, AND LOVERS, CLOSE AND WERE OF KEN, AND DEATH OF DREAM,
I WAKE. AND DAYLIGHT DAWN.

WHICH DREAM, I WONDER, WILL THE BETTER BE,
THE PILLOW SLEEP, OR FINAL DOZING FEAT,
WHERE PALL, AND PURPLE CLOTH, JOIN, CROSS THE STYX,
AND SANDMAN CALLS THE REAPER WITHOUT FEE.

(Balbriggan 1992)

ST. PHILOMENA'S CRIB [12]

THERE'S ONLY A BABY IN THE MANGER,
ONLY A BABY BOY, IN THE CRIB.
THIS SNOWY WHITE PURE CHRISTMAS TIDE.
JESUS, YOUR FATHER AND MOTHER,
YOUR SHEPHERDS AND ANGELS, ALL GONE,
NOT HERE IN THE CAVE,
A HOME-ALONE BABE.

ABANDONED, ALONE, THE CROSS IS NOW,
IN YOUR LITTLE MANGER.
ALONE WITH NONE BUT THEE MY GOD,
PHILO, LOVER ABANDONED
QUELLE ABANDON,
DE MYTHIFIED YOUR MUM
DE MYTHIFIED YOUR DAD.

(Palmerstown 1994))

BLACK AND CLERICAL, A PRIEST DOG

Luther, Author's Border collie.

BOUNDING DOG[13]

HIND LEGS, SWIFT PUSH, FORWARD,
EVEN WHEN RESTING AND HIS HEAD,
HUNG DOG, OVER SOFA,
PUSHING CUSHION AWAY, TO EARTH
HIS COMFORT.
DROPPING HEAD, AND SLOW PACE, ON SIGHT OF
OTHER.
YOU ARE BOSS DOG,
HAUGHTY SAVED DOG,
AND YOU KNOW YOU DESERVE THUS.

OFF THE STREET, WITH RAGGEDNESS
AND BLOODSHOT EYE,
SOME YEARS PAST,
TO PRIEST HOUSE,
YOUR FASTING OVER,
PARADISE REGAINED.

AT THE SOUND OF CHILDREN, EARS UP,
AT DOGS GROWL, BACK, AND
YOU ARE BOSS DOG.
A COMFORT, TRICKSTER AND FRAUD, IN
LUTHER, A REBEL, AND COCKSURE OF YOU.

BLACK AND CLERICAL, A PRIEST DOG,
AND PULLING NORA, WALKING TO RUN,
AND AT TEN THIRTY UP THE STAIRS
TO YOUR SKY-LIT DUVET.

SHAKE YOURSELF, AND READY TO RUMBLE,
TO YOUR GRANNY, AUNTIES AND
CHOICE CUTS,
NOTHING LESS,
YOUR FASTING OVER,
PARADISE REGAINED.

IN PARADISE WHERE BIRDS FLY FREE,
YOU WILL LIE, COMFORT EARTHED
UNDER THE TREE IN THE GARDEN
OF EDEN, WITH EYES ON THE GATE.

(Dundrum 1998)

THE QUARTER DIAMOND
(for 15th anniversary)

LYING PROSTRATE, ON A MARBLE SLAB
OF PRAYER, AND INCENSE, AND
SMOKING CANDLES.
BENEATH THE ORDINARY FEET,
A FETE OF FEATS ACHIEVED.

IN ST. ANDREW'S CHURCH BY HIS DECREE,
THE HOLY SPIRIT CAME
AND DWELT, IN PROMISE FROM ABOVE.
ON MOTHER'S TEARS AND FATHER'S COINS
IN AUNTIE'S HATS AND
GRANNY'S BEADS
TO HONOUR COMMITMENT,
ON A MARBLE SLAB.

"GIVE US YOUR BLESSING, FATHER",
"SAY A MASS, FATHER",
SIMPLE PIETY, AND GOD'S MOTHER
REFRACT, THIS QUARTER DIAMOND
A JEWEL, SMALL,
IN GOD'S TIARA.

(Palmerstown 1994)

A T.V. PERSONALITY

HE IS A T.V. PERSONALITY,
ONCE A WEEK ON AIR.
WE SIT AND LISTEN TO HIS VIEWS,
THROUGH BOUNCED QUESTIONS.
ON THE STREET WE SAY,
"LOOK, THERE'S A T.V. PERSONALITY".

HE OPENS CLUBS AND COFFEE BARS,
COLLECTS HIS CHEQUE AND GOES,
BECAUSE HE HAS A T.V. PERSONALITY,
ONCE A WEEK ON AIR.

"I COLLECT THE DOLE IN THE SAME OFFICE,
AS HIS WIFE'S SISTER'S HUSBAND."

IN WINTER HE WEARS SUN GLASSES,
BECAUSE HE IS A T.V. PERSONALITY.

JOHNNY, WHEN YOU GROW UP,
WILL YOU BE LIKE DADDY,
A T.V. PERSONALITY.
DO ALL TV'S HAVE PERSONALITY.

(Balbriggan 1992)

PEARL MERRYWEATHER

I sometimes see you on a bicycle,
with a basket in front,
or in a troublesome tangerine mini car,
needing to be pushed,
the car not you.
Nobody ever pushes you,
and if they did,
they soon learned,
they shouldn't,
and didn't,
again.
Push you,
only your mini.

You read in church,
sat in church,
and typed for church and sang
and prayed,
and paid in church.

"Nobody pushes, Dervilas only push the car",
now separated and divorced
from reality.
Slowly,
ever slowly,
reality dawns,
the vision wearing thin.
The world it too says,
nobody pushes,
and pays their dues.

(Balbriggan 1993)

NUN

TALL AND BLACK LADIES OF PRAYER,
STILL IN THEIR WHITE
BONNETS OF CARE,
MOTHERS AND SISTERS,
TENSE POLITENESS,
GRACEFILLED HUMOUR
OF MOTHERING HENS,
IN A COOP OF GRACE.

WITNESS OF LOVE,
BUT NEVER A MOTHER,
ONLY STEELED IN RESERVE OF CARE,
FUSS OVER FATHER'S EGG
AND OLD MRS PENNY'S HEALTH,

HAVE YOU CHANNELLED YOUR LOVE
ON THE VIA DOLOROSA,
SISTER ANGELICUS BONAVENTURA.

(Balbriggan 1992)

IN THE EVENING CORNER

Garden at Sweetmount Drive, Dundrum.

PARADISE GARDEN[14]

IN THE EVENING CORNER,
THE PRIEST'S GARDEN, SHOULDERED BY
COMPASSION, DUBLIN BAY,
AGATHA CHRISTIE AND MADAME
GREGOIRE STRACHEN.

I SMELL THE NEIGHBOUR'S EVENING SACRIFICE
OF BAR.B.Q MEAT SKEWERED.
ITS SMELL INCENSING THE SKY ABOVE.

GOD'S CUMULUS CRYING,
IN THE ROOF OF THE SKY,
LIKE EXTERNALISED HUMAN MOODS.
IT TOO BLOWS OVER.
DARKLY LUTHER'S HEAD LOOKS UP
AND THUNDER AWAITS,
THE FIREWORKS OF NOISE.

ROSE JUBILEE, SEXY REXY, AND
TEQUILA SUNRISE,
NORA'S GREEN-FINGERED HAND,
LIKE CHILDREN IN THEIR GRADE,

REMAINING HEADS SHOWING
THEIR LAST BLOOM.
IN THE CORNER, OF THIS,
THE GARDEN'S SOUL.

(Palmerstown 1996)

THE STEADY EBBING OF THE TIDE

Balbriggan Beach, North Dublin.

NATURE'S GRACES

HAVE YOU EVER THOUGHT
HOW PURPOSEFUL THE BIRDS FLIGHT HOME IS,
THE STEADY EBBING OF THE TIDE,
AND HESITANT FALLING OF THE
AUTUMN LEAVES?
ALL CYCLES, CHARTED, COMPLETE,
IN ONE EVENING GLANCE,
TOWARDS THE END OF SUMMER.

THE SOUND IN SKIES OF PLANES
AND TRAILING JETS,
TAKING HOME TO SUN,
THOSE SEARCHING ACHING HEARTS.
PRESENT ALL,
IN THIS HOMEWARD WORLD,
SIT DOWN AND SEE AND REST
IN GOD'S PLANNED HAND.

(Manresa 1995).

CHRIST WALKS ON ICY WATERS NOW

APPROACHING WINTER

A TUNNEL FEEL COMES DOWN TO US,
A SHAPELESS FEEL, TO GROUND.
THOUGH LIFE MOVES ON AS CYCLICAL
THE DARKNESS BACKDROP GROUNDS.

THE ACTORS, LINES AND EPILOGUE,
WILL WAIT FOR WINTER CHILL,
TO TASTE, TO FEEL,
TO GET A COLD, AND IN COME
 PLANTS FROM SILL.

THE TEMPERATURE IS FIFTY NOW,
AND GOING DOWN AT NIGHT,
WHILE ISTANBUL IS EIGHTY-TWO,
GIVES SOUL THAT DIFFERENT LIGHT.

YET CHRIST HE ROSE,
ON THAT THIRD DAY,
FROM EVENING FADING LIGHT,
WE ACTORS WAIT, THE CURTAIN CALL,
AN ENCORE SUMMERS NIGHT.

LIFT UP YOUR SOUL,
IGNORE THE CHILL,
IT GETS MUCH WORSE THAT THIS,
TO THINK IT OUT, WILL KILL THE WILL
AND BODY PAIN, WILL STILL FALL ILL.

CHRIST WALKS ON ICY WATERS NOW
AND LEADS US THROUGH THE CHILL
WHERE TEMPERATURES MIGHT RAISE WITHIN
AND LAST ALL NIGHT AND CARRY SOUL
UNTIL WE RISE IN SPRING.

(Balbriggan 1993)

AND WHEN I CROSS THE RIVER STYX

BOATMAN FROM THE RIVER STYX

SOMETIMES WE HEAR THE BOATMAN'S CALL,
TO GO AND WALK TO RIVER BOAT,
AND STEP ABOARD THE FERIBOT,
AND CROSS THE STYX
AND PAY THE TOLL.

FOR NOW I HEAR THE BELL ITS TOLL,
IS SLOWER, PEALING, LOUDER STILL,
BETWEEN THE SILENCE AND THE EVE,
THE TOLL PEALS ON AND ON.

PERHAPS GOOD-BYE'S A SAD REFRAIN
AND BORROWED FUN FROM FRIENDSHIP LEFT,
RECALL THE JOY AND HAPPY DAYS
BEFORE WE CROSS THE RIVER STYX.

IT WAS A GLIMPSE AND ENDED FAST
TO SHOW PERHAPS THAT LOVE CAN'T LAST,
THIS SIDE,
WITHOUT THE TOLL BEING PAID.

THE EVENING DARKENS SOON,
THE BELL, IT PEALS FAR ON PAST NOON,
WHERE FURROWS DEEPLY DUG
AND PLANTED GRAPES,
MIGHT YIELD A WINE
SO WHITE.

AND WHEN I CROSS THE RIVER STYX,
I HOPE MY LORD WILL COME WITH ME,
AND HELP ME INTO BYZANTINE,
AND SEE THE FACE OF HIS IN MINE.

AND THEN I WILL BE HOME AGAIN,
MY JOURNEY'S END RETURN,
WHERE EDEN IS SO EASTERN,
AND LIFE IS NOT FORLORN:

FOR WHEN YOU GIVE YOUR HEART THEN

I AM AFRAID, THE BELL, IT RINGS,
FOR EACH TO STAND AND GO,
AND LEAVE THE ONES THAT
WE HAVE KNOWN,
AND PLAYED WITH IN SOJOURN.

DO NOT BE SAD TO HEAR THE BELL,
AND DO NOT RUN AWAY,
THE BOAT IS DOCKED AND BOARD IT NOW
FOR SOON IT ROWS PAST MALL.

IN ISTANBUL THE BIRDS FLY FREE,
AND WINE THAT CHILLED IS KIND,
THE RIVER PULLS IN PAST THE LINE
PAST DOLMEBACHE AND TREE.

YOU TOO WILL MAKE A JOURNEY THERE,
ACROSS YOUR RIVER STYX,
SO GATHER FAST THE TOLL AND FIND
THE PASSAGE WAY THAT'S YOURS.

FOR WHEN YOU GIVE YOUR HEART THEN,
THE TOLL BEGINS TO SOUND,
AND WATCH THE HOVERING VULTURES
MOVE, STEALTHILY TOWARDS THE GROUND.

IT IS NOT SAFE TO FALL IN LOVE,
LEST LONELY HEARTS GO MAD
WITH RAGING PULSE,
AND CRAZY MIND,
CAN STEAL THE POUNDING DOVE.

O THETIS[15] DIP MY FEET IN STYX,
AND STRENGTHEN MY RESOLVE
AND DRINK THE NECTAR SWEET.
ACHILLES' HEEL IS SORE NO MORE
ADONIS CURED ITS FEET.

BE NOT AFRAID O TRAVELLER GO,
AND VIEW YOUR ROADS IN LIFE,
LET THE REAPER GO TO HELL,
HIS GRIMNESS HOLDS NO CHILL.

(Istanbul 1992)

*AROUSE THE STRENGTH
TO CHANGE THE WAY*

WHEN EARTH WAS KISSED BY MARS

COME CLOSE DEAR MARS
SO CLOSE TO EARTH,
THE HUNDRED YEARS IS HERE,
YOUR SUBJECTS HAVE ATTRACTED YOU,
YOU COME TO LOOK, AND SEE.

YOUR LOOK AT EARTH IS VENUS LIKE,
AS HOMER TOLD IN ODE,
WHAT CALLS YOU NOW,
YOUR SUBJECTS OR YOUR LOVE?

YOUR FIERY RED ATTRACTS OUR GAZE,
ON OUR HORIZON VIEW,
A PRODUCT OF A FLOWER LOVE,
OR HONEY NECTARED DEW.

IS IT EMIGRATION, WAR,
OR SAD RELIGIOUS STRIFE,
WHERE ENMITY IS CONSTANT FARE,
ON EARTH'S DULL POLITY.

AWAKEN GODS YOUR COURAGE SONS,
AND NOT SUBSERVIENT CHILD,

AROUSE THE STRENGTH,
TO CHANGE THE WAY,
SO EARTH IS KISSED BY MARS.

(Istanbul 1992)

CUT THROUGH THE MARMARA WAVES

(Top) Haghia Sophia, Istanbul.
(Bottom) Topkapi, Ottoman Palace, Istanbul.

MARMARA[16] DANCE

SAIL ON PAST,
PAST TOPKAPI AND DOLMABACHE[17],
SAIL ON, UNDER LIGHTENING SKY,
TO FRENZIED MUSIC.

ON LIKE A FRENZIED STALLION,
ORIENTAL SHIP,
UNDER THUNDER MOON,
DANCING TURKS,
TO ORIENTAL MUSIC,
SHARP AND SENSUOUS.

CUT THROUGH THE MARMARA WAVES,
POWERFUL BOAT, THRUSTING WAVES,
CARRYING EXCITED LIFE,
UNCARING, BUT FOR LIFE AND JOY,
ROMANTIC SOUND, AND BODY SWAYS,
DARK-HAIRED DANCING WOMEN,
AND SLEEK LEVANTINE MEN.

(Istanbul 1992)

MY MOTHER'S LIFE WAS FULL OF PRAYERS
Alice Hughes, pictured in Rathfarnham 1960.

FROM DUNMORE EAST
The author's parents (c. 1950) at Dunmore East.

PINK HYDRANGEA BLOOM

THESE ARE THE DAYS THAT I WILL CHERISH,
IN MY MOTHER'S GARDEN CHAIR,
REST BETWEEN LABURNUM TREES,
THAT FACE ACROSS THE SISTER FLOWER.

TIME GOES FAST IN SUMMER BREEZE,
WHERE LEISURE CAN BE FREE,
TO THINK AND SIT, AND LET WORK PERISH.

SHE WOULD PUT TEA LEAVES UNDER FLOWERS
OF HYDRANGEAS FROM DUNMORE EAST,
THAT ONLY BLOOMED, NOT FLOWERED.
AND SHAKE THE EARWIGS FROM THE MOP,
BEFORE THE KITCHEN FLOOR WAS DONE.
AND SMILE WITH PRIDE AT HER ROSES,
GROWING FULL FOR FORTY YEARS,
ALONG THE COALHOUSE WALL.
A LIGHT PINK,
A SLIP NOW GROWING
IN THE PRESBYTERY GARDEN.

THESE ARE THE DAYS THAT I WILL CHERISH,
BETWEEN BLOOM AND FLOWER,
THE ROSE AND HYDRANGEA GARDEN,
BETWEEN LIFE AND ETERNITY.

MY MOTHER'S LIFE WAS FULL OF PRAYERS,
AND BISHOPS THOUGHTS AND COUNTRY LIFE,
AND SAYINGS LEARNT LONG AGO,
BETWEEN THE FLOWER AND THE BLOOM.

(Rathfarnham 1993)

One of Hermes' functions was to be the messenger of the gods; this Greek bronze statue shows him resting and wearing the winged sandals which were his attributes. Naples, National Museum.

NOT GOTHIC, NOR DULL
Hermes, God's Messenger.

Heracles' final Labour was to bring the golden apples from the Garden of the Hesperides to Eurystheus. Antique relief showing Heracles seated under the trees bearing the apples, guarded by the dragon Ladon. Rome, Villa Albani.

BUT PRIMEVAL, NATURE'S WAY
Heracles, under apple tree.

LAUGHTER

LAUGHTER IS RED AND ROSY,
ROUND AND WHOLE,
SQUEEZING, SWEATING, OIL OF JOY,
FROM SEDATE, DESCRIBED LIVES.
RED AND ROSY,
OVERCOMING GREY SHARPNESS,
LAUGHTER IS ROMANESQUE,
AND LOVELY,
NOT GOTHIC, NOR DULL,
BUT PRIMEVAL NATURE'S WAY,
OF OLIVE OIL.

(Rathfarnham 1991)

Francis Albert Sinatra

Born Into Life December 12, 1915
Entered Into Eternal Life May 14, 1998

OLD BLUE EYES
(Poem to Sinatra)

HE WAS HUNGRY FOR DINNER AT EIGHT,
AND SWAGGERED ONTO TO MUSIC STAGE,
WITH AUDIENCES EAGERED FOR SONG,
AND PRESENCE OF THE CONFIDENT MASTER OF CONTROL,
IN LIFE AND FILM AND LEGEND.
FROM BLACK-HAIRED YOUTH TO GREY OLD MAN,
A COLOSSUS, WHO COULD
MAKE IT THERE AND ANYWHERE,
IT WAS UP TO HIM.

WOMEN'S LOVE FILLED THAT NEED
OF AFFECTION AND
MEN THE SALOON CHUMS,
SONG GATHERED THE EYES OF
THE BLUE SEA OF ADMIRATION,
FROM SIXTY YEARS,
THROUGH CINEMA AND SONG.

WHEN YOUR AWAITED DEATH,
BROKE ON SKY,
THE TRIBUTES RECALLED
EVERYBODY'S YEARS,
EVERYBODY'S EMOTIONS AND
ROMANTIC LOVES,
THE HEART OF LIVING,
FANTASY AND ROMANCE
WERE STATUED BY YOU.
YOUR TUXEDO APPROACH TO LIFE
SEALED THOSE MOMENTS IN
THE ACCEPTABLE WORLD,
NO LONGER PRIVATE,
AND THAT'S LIFE.

He's alone in a crowd — perfectly alone.

YOU WERE PUPPET, PAUPER,
AND KING OF THE HILL,
AND LIVING WAS UNDERLINED AS
YOUR WAY, AND LOOKING DEATH
AS A CONTRACT ON YOU,
AND YOU AT THE BAR, TO LOOK
IN THE EYE,
THE GRIM REAPER.

PUT AWAY THE CALENDAR, THE VINYL,
THE MAGAZINES AND FASHION,
HANG UP THE TUXEDO,
SINK THE DANIELS AND CAMEL,
AND START ALL OVER AGAIN.
THE BAR IS NOW CLOSED,
THE CONCERT HALL EMPTY,
THE TRIBUTES ALL OVER,
SO LONG SALOON MAN,
ADIOS AMIGOS,
HOLLYWOOD, TAKE DOWN YOUR SIGN,
AND BLUE EYES,
SHINE,
IN THE BIG CASINO.

(Dundrum 1998)

SLOE BUSH

WALKING BY AS CHILDREN,
WITH MY FATHER STRIDING ON.
WE STOPPED AND TASTED SOURNESS,
ON THE BUSH AT WHITECHURCH LAWN.

SLOE SORBETS OUTSIDE THE VICAR'S GATE
AND GREEN AND FERNY MOUNTAIN
CALLS WAY UP AHEAD.

RATHFARNHAM WAS A COUNTRY PLACE
OF WALKS AND ROADS AND SHRUBS
IN GARDENS VYING, PAST WHITECHURCH,
ROUND COLUMBA'S COLLEGE FACE.

PINK FERNY COLOURED MOUNTAIN CALL,
FOR FEET TO TEST AND VIEW,
THE LAND, BELOW, THIS THRONE OF GRACE,
OF NATURE'S CARPETS BLUE.

THERE'S NOTHING LIKE A WOODED WALK,
IN KILMASHOGUE'S GREEN BELT,
WHERE NATURE'S FREEDOM KISSES HEALTH,
AND DANCE- LIKE STYLE, IN TÍR NA NÓG.

THIS HILL IS WITH A HIGH PRIESTS CHAIR,
AND NATURES GARMENTS SHEDDING BARE,
IN WINTER, YET, IT'S DOWN BELOW
THAT TAKES ITS STYLE FROM HERE.

(Rathfarnham 1991)

THE CAT, IT DARED TO STARE AFAR

THE CAT AND THE STARLING

BETWEEN ITS TEETH, THE WICKED CAT,
HAD CAUGHT THE BIRD LIKE A CRICKET BAT,
AND RESCUED BY MY MOTHER'S STICK,
STAYED FRIGHTENED BY THE UNWELCOME LICK.

THE CAT IT DARED TO STARE AFAR,
AS IF ITS PRIZE WAS A FALLING STAR,
AN ANGRY FACE AND WICKED GLARE,
SHOWED ITS ANGRY SOUL WAS BARE.

LIKE COURSING MEN, IT SEEMS WE OWN,
A LOVE FOR KILLING NATURES OWN,
WHERE RED-FACED HUNTING MEN WILL GATHER
THE CAT HAD WELL ENJOYED THE BATTER.

THIS ORIGINAL SIN IN ALL IS BUILT,
BENEATH OUR SOUL IT LIES LIKE SILT,
THE GRACE OF GOD AND LIFE'S LONG LESSON,
AT TWILIGHT BECOMES THE JUDGEMENT SESSION.

(Rathfarnham 1991)

*HOW DO YOU STAND SO ERECT,
AND STILL, IN THE HEAT OF THE DAY?*

ATATURK[18] SOLDIER

HOW DO YOU STAND SO ERECT,
AND STILL, IN THE HEAT OF THE DAY?
SOLDIER OF DOLMABACHE AT YOUR GATE,
GUARDING WITH DIGNITY YOUR PALACE.

HOW DO YOU STAND SO STILL,
ONLY A BEAD OF SWEAT CAN MOVE,
DOWN YOUR CORRECT, DIRECT STARE,
AT THE GATES OF THE SULTAN'S HOUSE?

HOW DO YOU REMAIN SO DIGNIFIED,
AND STILL LIKE, AS THE CLOCKS WITHIN,
THAT MARK THE PASSING OF A HERO STATESMAN?
STILL AND SILENT.

TOURIST OF EUROPE,
STAND BESIDE YOU,
AND WONDER AT YOUR POISE,
LIKE THE TURK, ERECT DIRECT,
STILL AND STRONG.

MARMARA BOATS THAT SAIL AND MOVE,
TOURISTS THEN MAY COME AND GO,
HAVE BEEN DIRECTED AND SMILE TO YOU,
AND WONDER HOW,
SOLDIER OF DOLMABACHE.

(Istanbul 1991)

THIS IS ISTANBUL

MINARETS AND MOSQUES

MINARETS AND MOSQUES,
SOUKS AND SHADOWS,
KEBAB SMELLS AND PERFUMED SPICE,
HOOTING SOUNDS AND NOISY DRIVERS,
SWEATING PALMS AND NECKS,
LEMON COLOGNE AND COLA,
THIS IS ISTANBUL.

ATATURK PICTURES, LOKANTA COUNTERS,
PROUD MEN, ACTIVE, MOVING,
GOING SOMEWHERE, BELLY DANCERS,
CROWDED BAZAAR,
THIS IS ISTANBUL.

CRIES OF "CHAI, CHAI, AYRAN, AYRAN[19]",
NO IGNORED MIRROR,
SARAP, TURNIP JUICE,
THIS IS ISTANBUL.

PIERRE LOTI YOU HAVE BEEN HERE,
THIS CITY IS AZIYADE,
LEVANTINE DARK AND
EVENING COMES
SMALL STREETS AND COBBLED STONE,
THIS IS ISTANBUL.

BUT ISTANBUL IS LOVE AND MAGIC,
PASTA TASTE AND RAKI,
WATCHING FROM A WINDOW
HAREM-LIKE, OR WIDOWED ON
PRINCE'S ISLE,
THIS IS ISTANBUL.

(Istanbul 1991)

FROM TRABZON TO GUMUSHANE

Trabzon costume, ancient Phrygian Dynasty.
King Gordion and King Midas ruled 8 BC.

FROM TRABZON TO GUMUSHANE

I TRAVELLED LIKE A SULTAN,
IN A CRAVAN ON WHEELS,
FROM TRABZON TO GUMUSHANE.

THE WEATHER SWEATED AND COOLED
THE BROW
AT STOPS A LONG THE LORDLY PEAKS,
OF ZIGANA PASS AND DAG.

AT CALIPHS STOPS, THE CAMELS HALT,
AND CHILDREN SAY HELLO,
AT TOURIST BRIGHT AND HEAVY CLOTHES
AT WHITENESS LILY SHOW,

OUR CARAVAN PASSED LIKE XENIPHON[20],
IN CONQUESTS TRAILS,
AND WHERE HIS MEN EMBRACED IN JOY
WE DRANK A COLA FROM A TIN.

(Istanbul 1992)

*IT WAS AN EVENING
YET LESS AN EVENING
THAN A STAGNANT DAWN.*

(Purgatorial Passions, Owen)

Wilfred Owen, poet of 1st World War.

BOMBED IN OMAGH

A FETID, PUTRID, ROTTEN, EVIL SMELL,
THAT STINKS THE NATION IN ITS CARNAGE
OF INNOCENT, OLD AND YOUNG,
SHOPPING ON SATURDAY AFTERNOON.
"WHAT WILL YOU BUY WITH YOUR POCKET MONEY",
"I MUST GET THAT BOYZONE OR SPICE GIRLS CD,
AND NEW UNIFORM FOR SCHOOL".
"I AM GETTING MY EYES TESTED, WON'T I LOOK GRAND,
IN THE NEW FRAMES, HE'LL HAVE THEM
READY ON SATURDAY."

SOMEONE DRIVES A CAR
AFTER HIS REPUBLICAN LUNCH,
THAT SAME SATURDAY, INTO OMAGH.
"WHAT ARE YOU GETTING, DADDY, IN THE TOWN,
WILL YOU BRING SOMETHING BACK, DADDY?"

SOMEONE IS SITTING THE WEEK BEFORE,
PLANNING THE STRATEGY, THE FINAL PUSH,
ONE MORE FOR ÉRIN GO BRÁTH,
WRAP THE GREEN FLAG ROUND ME BOYS,
A NATION ONCE AGAIN.
GOD SAVE IRELAND, INDEED.

MAYBE YOUR WORDS DID SEND THEM OUT,
SENATOR YEATS,
AND THOSE WHO MADE YOU SENATOR TOO.
MARCHING TO THE GENERAL POST OFFICE
WASN'T A GREAT START, AN OMAGH TOO.
BLOODY SUNDAY, BLOODY SUNDAY,
SUNDAY BLOODY SUNDAY,
AND BLOODY SATURDAY AS WELL.

IS GENERAL CUSTER ON HIS LAST STAND,
OR IS A PATRIOT A TERRORIST, FASCIST,
WHO TELLS THE PEOPLE,
THE MAJORITY, "YOU HAVE NO
RIGHT TO BE WRONG"?

BRITISH SOLDIERS AMBUSHED,
STRIPPED NAKED FOR THE WORLD,
AND ONLY A PRIEST TO OFFER TRUTH,
A NATION ONCE AGAIN.

GOD SAVE IRELAND,
WEAR THE GREEN ON PADDY'S DAY,
SING THE SONGS OF BLOOD-CURDLING CRY
AND MEN BEHIND THE WIRE.
BAN THE BRITISH FROM HURLING,
UNTIL THE FOURTH GREEN FIELD,
IS A NATION ONCE AGAIN,
IRELAND UNFREE, AND ALL THAT.

"WHAT WILL I GET WHEN I GO INTO TOWN
THIS SATURDAY AFTERNOON?
WHAT ARE YOU PACKING SO CAREFULLY
IN YOUR CAR, DADDY?"

AND WE ALL SIGN THE BOOK
AND SEND THE FLOWERS,
AND STAND FOR THE MINUTE,
AND POLITICIANS
LOOK GRIM AND SHAKE HANDS,
"WHAT ARE YOU PACKING IN YOUR WORD,
AND DEEDS,
YOUR STIRRING, VOTE-CATCHING
SPEECH?"

DO YOU STAND FOR THE BLAST?
DO MY WORDS SEND THEM OUT?

GOD SAVE IRELAND.

(Dundrum 1998)

OF TENDERNESS AND YOUTHFUL ARMS

IT IS ONLY WITH THE HEART THAT ONE CAN SEE RIGHTLY;
WHAT IS ESSENTIAL IS INVISIBLE TO THE EYE.

Antoine de Saint-Exupery

DARK LOVER IN THE SONNET[21]

SVELTE LOVE WITH YOUR AMOROUS CHARMS
OF TENDERNESS AND YOUTHFUL ARMS,

THIN AND COLOURFUL THROW OF SMILE,
ALL SHINING, LOVELY, WAIT A WHILE.
FOR HONEST, TRUTH AND AURA LOVE,
COMES THROUGH YOUR BEAUTY, RADIANT DOVE,
OF INTUITIONS PERCEPTIVE EYE,
A CAUTIOUS, WAITING, LOVE NOT SHY.

WRAP AROUND ME YOUR CHARMS OF LIFE,
YOUR SURE AND UNDERSTANDING DOOR,
AN ENTRY OUT OF BILIOUS STRIFE,
A LOVE BEYOND A DEEPEST CORE,
AND THIS IS LOVE, OUR HUMAN REACH,
THAT ONLY GROWING OLD CAN TEACH.

(Dundrum 1998)

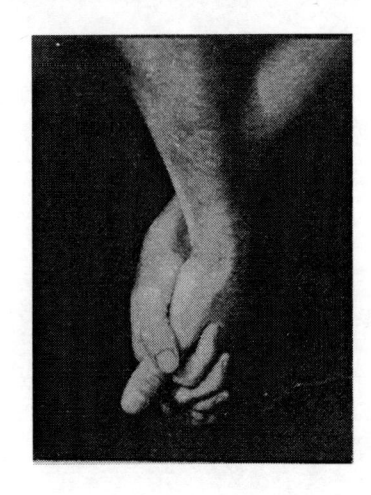

SEPTEMBER MORN
(To my mother, Alice)

AS YOU LIE THERE, FLAT AS A PANCAKE,
STILL SHARP AS A BIRD,
I THINK OF YOUR ACTIVITY OF LIFE,
NOT AN OLD GREY-HEADED WOMAN.

YOUR BLACK HEAD THROWN BACK IN
LOUD LAUGHTER,
THOUGH YOUR LIFE WAS HARD,
WITH ARTHRITIS, AND WORK
AND OTHER THINGS TOO.
GOD WAS ALL IN ALL,

THAT'S WHAT FR. PRENDERGAST, S.J. SAID
AT THE WOMEN'S SODALITY AND
THE FIRST WEEK OF THE WOMEN'S RETREAT
ORGANISED BY CANON O'DONNELL, P.P.
YOUR DESIRE TO BE A NUN WAS SQUASHED,
BUT THE SAME FAITH IN GOD'S
EXISTENCE WAS TRUE FOR YOU
AND TO YOU, A SIXTH WAY,
AQUINAS, EAT YOUR HEART OUT,
EXISTENTIALLY, THROUGH PRAYER.

I REMEMBER THE SMELL OF APPLE JAM, AND
BROWN BREAD FRESH WITH SCONES,
SOME TO SR. CANICE AND OTHERS TO
JESUIT VISITORS FROM THE CASTLE, AND
FR. STEPHENSON, S.J., TREADING THE WINEPRESS,
MADE OF HIS APPLES,
PATRICK KAVANAGH SPOKE WITH YOU ON THE SEAT
REMINISCING,
AN OASIS OF FARMLAND IN DUBLIN'S
RAGLAN ROAD.
AND FR. KENNEDY, S.J., ABOUT HIS ORNITHOLOGY,
AND BULL ISLAND,
YET NO BULL WITH YOU.

JESUIT VISITORS FROM THE CASTLE

Fr Stephenson. S.J., author of 'Treading the Winepress'.
Pictured with author at Rathfarnham Castle, 1971.

YOUR EPISCOPAL PEERAGE WAS BLUE,
AND YOU KNEW A FRIEND ON THE TITANIC,
AND MARGARET PEARSE CHATTED,
THAT'S A LIFE, RELIGIOUS AND
HISTORICAL,
AND SO YOU CAN BE ALIVE,
NOT GREY AND OLD AND FLAT
AS A PANCAKE,
WITH ALL THOSE MEMORIES WITHIN,
TO FLOWER IN THE SUN OF TRUTH.

JUSTICE AND TRUTH, STRAIGHT,
NO GREY, THOUGH,
HARD LIFE MEANT YOU COULD SEE THROUGH THE
FOOLISH,
AND FAITH GAVE YOU THE DIRECTION.

THERE COULD BE JOY IN SORROW,
WHEN GOD SHINES,
ON OUR LADY'S BIRTHDAY, ST. PHILOMENA'S
CHORD,
PADRE PIO, AND
ALL THE ARTEFACTS OF RELIGION,

YOUR EPISCOPAL LINE WAS BLUE

Bernard O'Reilly, granduncle of Alice Hughes.
Bishop of Harford, Connecticut, 1850.
Died on sinking ship 1856 between Liverpool and U.S.

HUGHES, JAMES (John and Alice O'Reilly) Rhyne. Born 5.11.1830. *Educated:* Moyne, France where he received minor orders from the Archbishop of Paris, Marie August Sibour, who was afterwards assassinated. He was ordained by his uncle, Bishop Bernard O'Reilly in Providence, Rhode Island, on 4.7.1852. *Appointments:* Secretary to his uncle and rector of the Cathedral, Professor in the Diocesan Seminary, Providence. In 1854 he became Pastor of St. Patricks Church, Hartford. He remained there until his death fifty one years later. In 1875 St. Patrick's old church was burned. Fr. Hughes immediately began the building of a new church. This task he completed in two years. It was dedicated in 1877. It has a seating capacity for over 2,000 people. He also built a convent, a school, a hospital and an orphanage. He established a burse in the North American College for the Education of a student in preparation for the priesthood in Hartford Diocese. He was Vicar-General of the Hartford Diocese for over thirty years. He died 7.8.1895 and his remains are interred in Hartford. When attending Moyne he stayed with his relations in Cunareen.

Vicar General James Hughes, uncle of Alice Hughes
also of Connecticut.

RHUBARB AND ROSES, FLOWER BEDS, AND
KNEELING TO TRIM THE GRASSY BORDERS,
"A JOB IS NOT FINISHED UNTIL
IT'S WELL DONE",
WE CANNOT KNOW THE HARSHNESS
OF MAKING SHEETS FROM
FLOWER SACKS,
AND MANGLING CLOTHES DRY,
IT MUST HAVE HAD A RESULT,
BUT FAITH WAS REAL.

NO COURSES IN SELF ESTEEM OR SEARCHING FOR
YOUR NUMBER ON THE ENNEAGRAM,
BUT HAPPINESS ON HEARING PAVAROTTI FROM
AMERICA WITH THE OTHER TWO,
OR FINBAR WRIGHT, DERMOT O'BRIEN
AND CÉILI HOUSE,
AN OASIS IN DUBLIN CITY.

ALTHOUGH FIFTY YEARS IN DUBLIN
KILLOE REMAINS YOUR VOICE AND
FAITH,
AND YOUR RECITATION OF BARBARA
FREITCHIE[22],
"UP FROM THE MEADOWS,
RICH WITH CORN,
COOL IN THE CLEAR SEPTEMBER MORN".

APPLE TARTS AND SANDRA ORANGE,
MUSIC AND FAITH,
NOT FLAT AS A PANCAKE,
THAT'S ONLY THE OUTER GARMENT,
BETWEEN HYDRANGEA FLOWER AND BLOOM,

CLEAR IN THE COOL
SEPTEMBER MORN.

(Dundrum 1998)

AND ISTANBUL, THE SAME

(Top) Süleymaniyé or Golden Horn.
(Bottom) Covered Bazaar, Istanbul.

ORTAKOY[23]

TEMPLE BAR, LATIN QUARTER, LEFT BANK,
EACH CITY HAS ITS ORTAKOY,
AND ISTANBUL THE SAME,
SHIPS CALL LIKE AT BUS STOPS
OR TRAINS IN VENICE
OR BOATS AT KADIKOY.

BERLEYBEYI LOOKS ACROSS,
FASHIONED LATINS
AND LADIES PARADE, NOT WALK,
A POET SELLS HIS BOOKS AT LITTLE TABLE
AND READS IF YOU WISH,
A PIERRE LOTI
SAN AZIYADE.

DISCOS SOUNDS OUT DONE.
BY WAVES
OF THE SEA AND
COLOURS OF THE CLOTHES OF
MODERN CALIPHS, CALLING IN CLOTH,
AND SOOTHE, SAY, SWIM,
EMOTION OF THE MARAMARA WAVE.

(Istanbul 1992)

A SCENE WITHOUT CARPETS

(Top) Sultan Ahmet III, Dining Room Topkapi Palace, Istanbul.
(Bottom) Alexander Sarcophagus, Archaeological Museum, Istanbul.

YENI KAPI[24]

A SCENE WITHOUT CARPETS,
FOR ROBERTSON'S BRUSH CANVAS,
ONLY THE SEA AND ROCKS AND MOORED
ORIENTAL BOATS, AND CHESTNUTS
CRACKLING IN HEAT WITH
CORN OF KOB.

PLEASURE OF AN HOUR IN HEAT STILL SUN
AFTER NOON ON LONG PROMENADE,
HUTS UNDER LEAVES AND CANVAS,
AND MAN-MADE SHELTER, A DEN OF BEARS,
AND FRESH, FISH, FRIED, FAST,

THE SEA, LIKE STILL JELLY,
MAKES A CARPET TO ITS CITY BACKDROP,
LOOKING ACROSS TOWARDS ISTANBUL,
LIKE ACROSS TO DALKEY FROM
A SHORE OF HEATED SHOES.

(Istanbul 1992)

AND CONIFER GOING GREEN AGAIN

Autumn scene.

TWO WEEKS OF RAIN

ANOTHER RAINED-OUT FORTNIGHT,
AND CONIFERS GOING GREEN AGAIN,
AND ROSES STARTING TO GO
ASLEEP, WITH
ENOUGH WATER FOR WINTER.

AND THEN THE SUN COMES PEERING OUT
BUT NOT YET, THE RAIN CLOUDS
AGAIN TAKE OVER.
WAIT LUTHER, YOUR WALK WILL COME,
AND BETWEEN DARK CLOUDS,
WE'LL GET A WALK
AND IN MARLAY PARK YOU CAN SNIFF
AWAY AT OTHER'S MARKS,
AND LEAVE YOUR ONLINE FAX.

AH. NOW THE SUN COMES OUT
AND WERE ALL THE HAPPIER,
EVEN IF ONLY MOMENTARY,
AND SMILING DOG OWNERS
LIKE PROUD PARENTS SMILE
 AS LUTHER PULLS AT THE LEASH
TOWARDS THEIRS,
A PATIENT, KNOWING SMILE.

AND IN AGAIN, THE CLOUD GATHERS,
BUT IT IS A SAFE PARK,
WITH LEASHED DOGS.
THE OTHER ONE AFTER PEARSE AND
DOWN THE ROAD, THE DOGGIES ROAM
AND FRIGHTEN KIDS, AND
STARTLE OTHER DOGS,
LAWS ARE GOOD AND ORDERLY,
WHEN PURPOSELY OBEYED.

Daedalus and Icarus whose wings
CAME APART IN THE HEAT OF SUN

*THE ORIGIN OF THE RISING
IS THERE SOMETHING IN THE AIR?*

Apollo ideal of beauty.

BEFORE ADMIRING YOU ADMIRING

IN THAT OTHER PLACE,
THE ORIGIN OF THE RISING,
POOR LUTHER AND HIS MASTER
GOT BITTEN,
THE OTHER MASTER SAYING
"HE'S NEVER DONE THAT BEFORE",
THERE IS ALWAYS
A 'NEVER DONE THAT BEFORE'.
AND SPEAKING TO THE CAPPED
GROUNDSMAN WHO KEEPS THE
DREAM OF PEARSE SAFE,
WITH HIS EYE ON THE CLOSING GATE-TIME,
"THERE IS NOTHING I CAN DO,
A BYE-LAW HARD TO ENFORCE,
AND PEOPLE DON'T OBEY IT ANYWAY".

IS THERE SOMETHING IN THE AIR
IN PEARSE'S DREAM,
BUT SAFER MARLAY, ORDERLY MARLAY,
ROUND THE LAKE AND WATCH THE DUCKS AND
GEESE,
AND NOW THE PROUD PEACOCK,
ADMIRING YOU ADMIRING,
AND SATURDAY MORNING
IS A SAFER PLACE?

(Dundrum 1998)

HAPPY PRIEST
(For Cardinal O'Fiach)

FROM MY PRIEST'S WINDOW
THE LARGEST HOUSE IN TOWN,
THE NORTHERN ROAD HAS BROUGHT
THE DEAD.
I SEE THE COMPASS ALWAYS NORTH.

GIBRALTAR THREE
HAVE PASSED THE HOUSE,
AND SMALL SCATTERING OF BLACK FLAGS
AND COAT BANDS.

THE STAINED GLASS CLARKE WINDOWS
HAVE SEEN REFRACTED LIGHT,
FROM CENTURIES, SHINING THROUGH,
YEARS PAST.
PETER AND PAUL WERE MARTYRS TOO.

AND HOMEWARDS TO THE BURIAL GROUND.

BUT THEN THE JOLLY, WHOLESOME,
SHINING CARDINAL PRIEST CAME BY,
AND A WHITE BAPTISMAL SHAWL ON HIS COFFIN.
SLOWLY PAST PLACES HE SPOKE IN GAELIC AND
HISTORY, AND FERGAL, IN HIS BLOOD.
AN HONEST, OUTSPOKEN, BROKER MAN,
WHO IN LONG KESH,
SOWED THE SEED OF THE PEACE WE
HONOUR NOW.

ALONG A ONE-WAY ROAD, A
NORTHERN CEMETRIED ROAD.
YET THE SEEDS HE SOWED, THE
PIPE SMOKING WITH GUSTY SPENCE,
WERE ACORNS OF THE OAK.

HIS LARGE KIND HEART,
BROKEN DEAD IN MARY'S PLACE
ABROAD.
MALACHY DIED ABROAD,
AND HIGH KINGS TOO,
A HIGH PRIEST YOU,
WHO SOWED THE SEEDS,
THAT GROW NOW, AND
HOME HE COMES,
AMONG FERMANAGH SPIRES.
PERHAPS THE GREY, STEEPLES
CAN RING OUT CHEER.

DULCE ET DECORUM EST,
PRO FIDE MORI.
A ATHAIR DHÍLIS.

(Balbriggan 1992)

LIKE A GHOSTLY SHROUD

Church of St. Gregory in Ani (former capital of Armenia)
and Ishak Pasha Castle, Dogubayazit, Turkey.

ANI[25]

LIKE A GHOSTLY SHROUD,
OF FLORENTINE STONE,
YOU STAND IN MAJESTY,
OUT FROM LOOSE EARTH
AND RUINS OF HISTORY,
FROM LAVA UPROAR.
A THOUSAND YEARS
YOUR PEOPLE RAN,
NOT TO BE ENSHROUDED
LIKE POMPEII.

YOUR CENTRE ATTRACTS TOURISTS,
TO THE TIGRIS, EUPHRATES SIDE,
YOUR HEAT, CONSCIOUSNESS,
RISE FROM GUN-POSTED BORDERS,
FIRM FROM CENTURIES OF STONE.

I STOOD AND WAS NEWGRANGED BY YOU,
EGYPTED BY YOU,
IN THE HEAT OF FRIENDS,
SITTING IN HOT HISTORY,
BUT ALWAYS AND FOREVER NOW,
FOR THE TRAVELLER.

(Ani 1987).

LIKE ANGELS' WORK, ISLAMIC STYLE

RUBILEV'S ICON

WITH DONOR KEBAB,
AND A CRUST OF MEATED BREAD,
WE SAT ON A STEP IN THE COOL
OF A BREEZE, SHOP DOOR STREET,
IN TRABZON[26] TURKEY COAST.

WE ARE THREE PRIESTS TRAVELLING,
FROM ROMAN THOUGHT TO MECCA CRY,
HUNGRY IN A SIDE STREET.

LIKE ANGELS' WORK, ISLAMIC STYLE,
OLD TESTAMENT FRIENDSHIP
SEATS US DOWN ON STOOLS OF CARE,
AND SHARES A GLASS OF WATER,
AN OLD MAN'S HOSPITALITY.

COULD GOD IN TRINITY,
GIVE AGAIN,
A CHILD TO SARAH,
OR WOULD SHE LAUGH.

(Trabzon 1987)

THE CRUCIFIXION

"WHAT A VIEW FROM UP HERE.
A CITY BELOW, A MAN AND TWO WOMEN
AT MY ALTAR OF SACRIFICE,
THE OTHERS SIMPLY WATCHING AND LOOKING."
LIKE THE MADAME WHO PRURIENTLY KNITTED IN
IN FRANCE WHILE A SACRIFICE ROLLED INTO A
BASKET.

THE STIGMATA ATTRACTS ITS BLOOD
THE RAW NAKEDNESS COVERED IN CHURCHES
AND GALLERIES FOR CENTURIES
FOR PRUDENCE SAKE.
PRUDENCE AND PRURIENCE
A FEAST OF THE VOYEUR
INEXTRICABLY LINKED IN THIS HILL OF CALVARY
LOOKING DOWN THE CITY SCAPE,
ITS HUMANNESS APPEALING.
LATER, I DON'T KNOW ANYMORE
IS IT AN ATTRACTION
A TABLOID PRESENTATION?
THEN IT WAS A MOTHER AND TWO FRIENDS.
THIS CRUCIFIXION, EVEN SIMON OF CYRENAS
COMMANDED.

(Balbriggan 1992)

WOODLAND WALK

I WALKED IN MY BARE FEET BARE, ON THE GRASS
OF CARPET LAIN UNDER THE SENSORS OF MY
BODY.
STALACTITES OF NATURE,
TICKLING MY FEET
WITH ITS MOIST DEWINESS
AND OPTICIANS' RESTFUL GREEN
ON THE HILLS OF KILMASHOGUE.

THE GAZE OF EYES ACROSS THE SCAPE,
THE CITY BELOW IN ITS HECTINESS,
AND FRENZIED BUSINESS,
SILENT IN DISTANCE LOOKING,
FROM MY EYES THE DISTANCE QUIET,
ON THE HILLS OF KILMASHOGUE.

AH, THE HILLS OF KILMASHOGUE
BREASTPLATE OF DUBLIN HILLS
THE SKY ABOVE, A DISTANCE TOO,
OF SOLITUDE, LOOKING DOWN, ON MY BUSY MIND
OF OBSERVATION
ITS VASTNESS WITH JET TRAILS IN THE SKY
AM I THE CITY TOO, FROM SKYVIEW
IS IT MORE PEACEFUL THERE,
IS IT MORE PEACEFUL THERE
ABOVE THE HILLS OF KILMASHOGUE,
ABOVE THESE HILLS, THESE BREASTPLATE HILLS
OF DUBLIN'S DESERT CALM?

(Rathfarnham 1990)

I WILL BE THE BIG BROTHER

MISE ÉIRE

MISE ÉIRE
MISE ÉIRE
MISE ÉIRE
MISE ÉIRE

CATHLEEN AND GAA
CHURCH AND STATE, AND
POLITICIANS AND CUTENESS
SAY THE WANTED THING.

I AM SHAPED OF A GEOGRAPHICAL DOG WITH
A COLONIAL MASTER NEAR, JOHN BULL.
I AM A TERRIER.
I BARK AND WHINE BUT AM IN NEED OF
MASTER MACGRATH.

LÁN DÓCHAS IS GRÁ

MISE ÉIRE IN EUROPE
OBEDIENT TO MY NEW MASTER.

I WILL ALWAYS BE DEPENDENT
AND WINDSWEPT AND AS ARAN IS TO ME
I WILL BE THE BIG BROTHER
BRITAIN AND EU AND US,

ALWAYS AN ECONOMICAL NEPHEW,
ALL ELSE IS POETIC FANTASY
MY INDEPENDENCE IN THE WORLD.

(Balbriggan 1990)

GOING HOME FAST, THE KIDS AND TEACHERS TOO.

Author 2nd from left at De La Salle, Churchtown, 1970.

SCHOOL

GOING HOME FAST, THE KIDS
AND TEACHERS TOO.
RUNNING SOME AND WALKING
FAST.
THE TEACHERS,
OTHERS IN STAFF ROOM
PUFFING STRESS AWAY
AND AGE EARLY OR VISIT
GRAVES OF THROMBOSIS.
   MOTHER OF SORROWS HEAR OUR
   SILENT PRAYER.

RUN STUDENT, RUN TEACHER,
RUN MINISTER,
JOHN IS RUNNING, SHEILA IS RUNNING
AND THE DOG TOO RUNS IN WELCOME
RUN RUN RUN.

THE MURDER MACHINE WILL CATCH YOU AND
TEACH YOU.

DEAR SAINT BINGO GIVE US HOPE
BLESSED LOTTO GIVE US FAITH
VENERABLE WHISKEY DROWN OUR SORROWS.

                                              (Balbriggan 1984)

IN ISTANBUL ON BAYRAM DAY

FOR BAYRAM

A LYRICAL MUEZZIN
MINARETS HIS MUSIC
TO ANNOUNCE
THE FIESTA
THE SLAUGHTER OF THE INNOCENTS.

CHOCOLATE SWEETS
TURKISH DELIGHT ON THE COUNTER OF THE SHOPS
AND CEYLAN CAFÉ BAR
ON ABDULHAKAMIT CAD
IN BELEDIYE DUKKANIARI
WHERE THE OWNER IS A PATRON OF THE ARTS
AND KUDRET WORKS FOR TURKISH LIRA
MAKING MARTINIS
SHINE IN DARKENED LIGHTS.

IT IS WELCOME THERE AND KIND
AND HELPFUL TO THE SOUL
AND FULL OF INDIVIDUALS
IN ISTANBUL ON BAYRAM DAY.

(Istanbul 1987)

THE CATALYST OF ATATURK

Kemal Ataturk.

A DRIVE ON FATIH BRIDGE

THE NECKLACE IN THE LINK CONTINUES
AS BRIDGE SPOTS
DIAMONDS IN THE NECKLACE
OF THE GOLDEN HORN.

GALATA FIRST IN LENGTH
GIVES WAY TO FATIH SULTAN MEHMET
IN DEMOCRAT FEAT OF EUROSTAR.

LINK EUROPE ASIA
THE CATALYST OF ATATURK
WAS FIFTY YEARS IN SPIRIT
AS LINKS IN CHAIN
JOIN WEST AND EAST
TO MAKE EURASIA.

(Istanbul 1987)

Antique relief showing Pegasus the winged horse, led by Bellerophon. Rome, Palazzo Spada.

FROM VAN IN THE AIR

Pegasus, whose feather fell to Tarsus, E. Turkey.

FROM VAN IN THE AIR

WOULD SHELLEY OR BYRON
KNOW THE GUN
ON THE ARM OF A SOLDIER
IN THE AIRPORT OF VAN.

TEA AND CARPETS CLOSE
TO THE EARTH
BUT BATTLE IN SKIES
EXCITES THE WAVES
AND SO A GUN POINTS TO THE AIR.

WHEN THE SCHOOL OF ATHENS FROM RAFFAELO
WAS PAINTED BOTH PLATO
AND ARISTOTLE
POINTED THE WAY.

THE GUN OR CARPET
CHANGES THE FACE
LIKE A MIRRORED WORLD
WITH POETS ON THE GROUND
AND POLITICIANS TRAVEL BY AIR.

LAKE VAN FROM THE AIR IS SMALL
AND SLOW
BUT RICH ON THE GROUND.

WELCOME BYRON AND SHELLEY
WHAT'S REAL REMAINS
AND IS SEEN BY THE TRAVELLER.

(Van 1987)

CALLING OUT MASS TO THE FAITHFUL,
WHO PARK CARS IN THE YARD

Old Mellifont, Co. Meath.

AUTUMN BENEDICTION

THE FIELDS ARE ON FIRE,
AT THE AUTUMN NIGHT SKY.
GREY AND LIGHT BLUE
A PASTEL MIX.
THOUGH MANET SAW
NOT THE IRISH COLOUR, OF
THE BEAUTIFUL NIGHT SKY.
IN THE CEILINGS OF TANNER'S WATERS
FROM THE PRIEST WINDOW
ON THE EDGE OF THE HOUSE.

I SEE DIFFERENT FIRES BURNING,
FROM THE FARMER'S FIELD
IN THE SAME SKY,
THROUGH THE TREES.

THEY BOW TOWARDS THE SOUTH
LIKE THE INCENSE THURIBLE,
OF THE THURIFER'S SWING
AT EVENING BENEDICTION,
IN THE OPEN AIR OF THE END
OF A DAY'S LAMENT,
AS IT BOWS TOWARDS GOD
IN THE EVENING OF TANNER'S WATERS AUTUMN.

THE EVENING BELL SOUNDS
CALLING OUT MASS TO THE FAITHFUL,
WHO PARK CARS IN THE YARD
TO OFFER TO GOD
THE SAME BENEDICTION AS THEY KNEEL,
AND HEAR THE APPEAL FOR ANCIENT MAYNOOTH
TO BE RESTORED.
LEST THE SWAY OF INCENSE SWAY,
AND BLOW INTO THE AUTUMN SKY,
ABOVE THE TANNER'S WATER.

(Balbriggan 1986)

LEAVES BROWN DOWN, YELLOW SAIL DOWN.

Manresa, Dublin, Autumn 1998.

LEAVES OF AUTUMN

CUT-BACK AMONG LEAVES OF AUTUMN,
SHEDDING NON-SELF, SHEDDING, SHEDDING.
AS LIKE DOG HAIRS, NO LONGER PURPOSEFUL.
FULLY, FULLY FALL, UNWASTED BEDDING,
FOR PLANTS AND GROWING THINGS.
PURPOSEFUL, PLACED, PICTURES,
POSITIONED, BLACK, WHITE, WHITE BLACK,
WITH OCEAN STORM OR CALM FOREST,
IT IS A PLACE OF SPIRITS, AND THEY
CAN HAVE THEIR HOURS IN NATURE.

MARTYRS FELLED AND FALLEN, LEAVES OF
AUTUMN,
BOUND DOWN, UNWASTED, USED AND USEFUL
STILL,
ETERNITY THEIR NEXT ADVANCE IN CYCLE MILL.

SELFISH, SELFLESS GRACE AND STILL MORE
GRACE IN SELF, AND THIS HOLY PLACE
OF HONES WINDOWS HONED SOULS.
IGNATION DARK CAVENESS[27] PROMPTING LIGHT
FROM SPIRIT IN THE ENTERING SELF
OF SAVED SOULS, SWEETENING SPIRIT,
YEASTING AND GESTATING IN HOLINESS SHEDDING,
AS BULBS IN DARK PLACE OF AUTUMN, FOR
SPRING.

LEAVES BROWN DOWN, YELLOW SAIL DOWN.
RED, RUSTED, RUSSET AND RUSTLE DOWN,
LEAVES GLIDE DOWN AND WHIRL SPIN DOWN,
BUT DOWN, DARK DOWN TOWARDS LIGHT.

WITHIN NATURE IS THE GREATEST BOUND,
OF WHAT CHRIST IS AND DOES GROUND,
IN MANRESA AND HOLY PLACE,
AS LEAVES OF AUTUMN.

(Manresa 1998)

SILENCE

THAT NAKED, NUANCED, EMPTIED TALK IS
SOUNDLESS.
IN WHICH WHAT IS, BECOMES, AND IS.
ITSELF, MOVES OUT TO FORM FROM SHAPES,
OF OTHER FORMING, NOISES WITHOUT SOUND.

IN SILENCE ELIJAH SENSED SHALOM WITH GOD,
NOT IN THE BUSTLING NOISE OF NATURE'S ODD
AND SPARKLING THUNDER FLASH AND BOOM,
AND INIGO FROM WITHIN THE CAVE OF GLOOM.
YET GOD MOVES DEEPER DOWN THAN CAVERN
TOMB.

SILENCE HEARS WITHIN, WHAT WILL BECOME,
AND SILENCE IS THE HUSHED RESPONSE OF SOME,
TO JOY AND LOVE AND SWEETEST SUNSET WONDER,
TO HEAR THAT SOUND IS BEINGS' OPEN THRUST.
AND LISTENING SILENCE SPROUTS THE SLEEP OF
JUST.
IN SILENCE, HEARTS SWELL, AND GREEN DOWN
DEEP.

(Manresa 1998)

OR MAGPIES GATHERING SILVER SHINING THINGS

THE GIANT OAK

THE GIANT GREAT GENTLE OAK IS THERE AND STAYS,
ITS SYNAPSE, NEURONS LINKED TO CENTRE EARTH
AND GROWS GREATLY, SLOWLY AS IT SHOULD,
AND DOES, BY BEING, THERE.

THINK HOW IF HUMAN-LIKE ITS MOVEMENT WENT,
AND NEVER ROOTED, SMALL AND SLOWLY STILL,
NO ACORNS, SHELTER OR BRANCHES SPROUT,
TO SHOW HOW GREAT THE EARTH'S STRONG SAP IS.

AND WHILE WE HUMANS GAD ABOUT LIKE FLIES,
OR MAGPIES, GATHERING SILVER SHINING THINGS,
THE OAK TREE IS, AND BEAUTY STATES ITSELF.
HOW EARTHED, STABLE GENIUS NEEDS TO GROW.

IT IS A THIEF OF BEAUTY, SNATCHED OF SOIL.
THIS SOLID, STAYING OAK THAT WELCOMES OUT,
ITS ARMS, OPEN, IN BRANCHED WELCOME,
ITS COSY UNDER-SHELTER, DROPPING SEEDS,
THE ROOTED THING IS EARTH'S NATIVITY.

(Manresa 1998)

EXCEPT TO GROW WITHIN OUR SOUL

ETERNAL SEEDS

AND TIME MOVES ON,
AND SHUFFLED FEET REST, MORE SOON,
AND GREYING TEMPLES, TEETH AND
FALLING HAIR, ALL WITNESS BEAUTY'S
TRANSIENT TIME.

AND BABIES CRY AND DOGS WILL BARK,
BUT PUPPIES TOO, GREY CHINNED,
GROW OLD, AND QUICKER, IN THEIR
SPAN OF SEVEN TO HUMAN ONE,
A CHEATING TRICK OF LIFE.

SO WHAT IS THEN?
EXCEPT TO GROW WITHIN OUR SOUL,
ETERNAL FRUITS THAT LIKE A STEM,
OR ACORN, SEED OUR GOODNESS DEED,
AND PROMPT FOR EACH, ETERNAL SEEDS.

AND SEE CHRIST'S ANGEL
OPEN BACK THE SHELL,
AND INTO LIFE, NO GREYING KNELL,
FOR CHRIST HIMSELF WALKS ON THE SWELL,
AND CHORUS SINGS IN ALLELUIA BELL.

(October 1998)

INTROIBO AD ALTARE DEI

THE MARKET PLACE
IS THE CENTRE OF
GOD'S HUMANNESS.

CONFESSIONS IN THE BOX
OF THE SNUG OF SHARED SIN
AND HEALING IS UNDERSTANDING
AS THE RIBALD LAUGH
OF THOUGHT EXPRESSED.

TOO SHAMEFUL IS THE SHRINE
TO SPEAK
AS THE MARBLE COLDNESS REFRACTING
CANDLE GLOW
REFRACTING MARBLE.

BILLY WAS A GREAT PRIEST
HE SWORE HE HEARD THE BEST CONFESSION
IN A CAB OF TRUCKS
AND SNUGS OF PUBS.

(Dublin 1988)

AFTER THE STORM

AFTER THE STORM COMES THE SILENCE OF HUSH,
THE CUT DEEP PEACE OF KNOWING MORE
AND A DEEPER KEN, DESCENT IS FORE,
KNOWLEDGE OF A PASTURE LUSH.

WHEN THE THUNDER BANGS, THUD AND CRASH,
AND LIGHTNING SPARKLES, FLASH SOUND, CRACK,
AND LOUDER BOTH, A STILL, LOUDER BLACK,
SCENE SKY, AND RAINS POUR, LASH.

AND IN THE HUMAN SPIRIT SPACE,
SAME TREMORS, NOISE AND RATTLE, SPLASH,
LIKE PAST AND FRIGHT AND SUDDEN TRASH,
EMERGE FROM LIGHTLY DARKENED CASE.

BUT WAIT, CHRIST BIDS YOU WALK TOWARDS HIM,
AND GRIPS YOUR HAND, AND MOVE FROM SIN,
TO FREEDOM, JOY FROM EMPTY DIN,
AND GROWTH OF SOUL, DEATHLESS STING[28].

(Manresa 1998)

ANGEL OF JABBOK

ALONE IN THE DARKNESS OF YOUR INNER FEEL,
AN ANGEL COMES FOR TESTING THE STEEL
OF YOUR SOUL, AND GOODNESS AND SAP THAT'S WITHIN,
AND SMITHY-LIKE, HONES AND CUTS SKIN.

PAUL'S CONSTANT ACHE OF LIMP OF SOUL,
WAS ECHO OF GOD NEED, HIS DRAWN-OUT ROLE,
AND YOUR JABBOK WRESTLE LEAVES YOU DRAWN
AND WAN, BUT GOD'S EDGE IS CLOSER TO DAWN.

THEY WRESTLED ALL NIGHT, AND THEIR HOLDS ARE TIGHT
AND JACOB'S HOLD[29] HELD TILL TO THE LIGHT,
OF MORNING, FOR THE ANGEL'S DAWN,
HAD LEFT THE MARK[30] AND LIMPNESS SPAWN.

O ANGEL OF JABBOK, YOUR JABBOK TOO,
IS A STRUGGLE TOWARDS CHRIST, AND WINS WITH YOU.

(Manresa 1998)

POOR FATHER SHAWN

POOR FATHER SHAWN, FOR MANY YEARS,
HAD SERVED HIS FLOCK THROUGH CHEER AND TEARS,
AND NOW WITH NO NEW SOULS TO FEED,
HE HAD NO PEWS TO TEND AND LEAD.

THE YOUNG THEY SANG IN PUBS AND PLAYED,
IN PARK FIELDS TILL THE SUN DID FADE,
NO OLD TO PIOUS PRAYERS DID COME,
FOR FEAR OF THIEVES, BEING OVERRUN.

HE CALLED TO DOORS, BUT ONLY SPOKE
ON STEPS, TO PEOPLE, MOVING FOLK
TO BUSY LIVES AND CLEARING DEBT,
HIS POOR OLD HEART WAS SADDENED YET.

NO FIRESIDE CHATS OR BUTTERED SCONES,
WITH COOLING JAM, NO CHAIRS LIKE THRONES,
BUT ONLY "CALL AGAIN PERHAPS,"
AND "YOU ARE AN AWFULLY GOOD OLD CHAP".

BY MANY NIGHTS, AND YEARS OF TOIL,
IN WINTER CHILL AND BOOTS WITH SOIL,
WITH ROVER, HIS OLD FAITHFUL DOG,
POOR FATHER SHAWN, THREW A FINAL LOG.

WHEN SADIE CALLED TO FIX HIS PLACE,
THE PRIEST, SHE SAW, HAD DIED IN GRACE,
HIS BEADS THEY LAY UPON THE FLOOR,
HIS DOG WAS HEARD TO BARK, NO MORE.

SHE TOOK THE DOG TO HER VERY HOME,
AND RANG HIS GRACE ON HER HUMBLE PHONE,
HIS PRIEST WITH CLICKING HEELS DID CALL,
AND AT A GLANCE DID MAKE THE PALL.

THE PEOPLE CAME AND PRAYED HIS MASS,
THE BISHOP SPOKE THAT LIFE DID PASS,
HIS PRIEST DID NOTE THE PRICE OF LAND,
AND SOLD THE HOUSE, THE CHURCH DID NOT STAND.

BUT ONE YOUNG MAN, WHEN FATHER SHAWN DID SPEAK,
IN GLORY DAYS OF PEWS AT PEAK,
WAS TOUCHED BY KINDNESS OF THE PRIEST,
AND GAVE HIS LIFE TO GOD, A CHRIOST.

NO LONGER, POOR OLD FATHER SHAWN,
IN HEAVEN WITH GOD AND ROVER SHONE,
THERE SITS ON A CARDINAL'S DESK IN ROME,
A PICTURE, DOG AND PRIEST FROM HOME.

AND UNDER THE FRAME IS WRITTEN SMALL,
"I HOPE YOU'RE HAPPY IN YOUR CALL,
HERE'S TEN POUNDS TO BUY A DRINK,
AND QUENCH YOUR THIRST, FROM PRAY AND THINK..

FOR ROVER'S GRAND, AND SADIE'S SPRIGHT,
YOUR SERVING MASS WAS ALWAYS RIGHT,
YOU WILL TRAVEL FAR, THE LADDER OF GRACE,
SAY PRAYERS FOR HOME, OUR LITTLE PLACE".

IT IS NOT THE BIG THAT GOD CREATES,
BUT LITTLE, SMALL, THAT GROWS HIS PACE,
FOR BETHLEHEM'S CAVE WAS OUT OF THE WAY,
BUT THERE IT WAS THAT GOD DID STAY.

AND IN YOUR HEART, DON'T WORRY, FRET,
IF YOUR FORTUNE IS ONLY THE FISHERMAN'S NET,
FOR CHRIST HIMSELF, KNOWS WELL THAT SHORE,
FOR HEAVEN IS OPENED THROUGH A SMALL HALF DOOR.

SO SAVOUR WELL THE SMALLEST OF GRACE,
THE LOVING HANDSHAKE, NOT THE GOLDEN MACE,
FOR CHRIST HE STROLLS THE DUSTY BACK ROAD,
WITH TWO, AND SHARES YOUR DWELLING BODE[31].

AT THE TABLE HE SAT AND SITS THERE STILL,
AND LIKE RUBILEV'S ICON[32] INVITES YOU IN,
TO SHARE AND STAY THE EVENING LATE,
AND ENOUGH IS THERE UPON HIS PLATE.

(Manresa 1998)

LUTHER DOG

WHO'S THIS CURLED AT MY HEEL IN BED?
HIS OUTSTRETCHED PAWS AND RESTING HEAD,
WEARING CLEAN WHITE SOCKS AND BIB ALL WHITE,
YES, LUTHER'S BLACK COAT IT SHINES BY LIGHT.

AT THE SOUND OF A CAT, FAST TO THE DOOR,
OR POSTMAN'S LETTERS CHEWED ON THE FLOOR,
AND NOISE THAT'S STRANGE WON'T PASS HIS EAR,
HIS LIVELY SOUL, GIVES ALL SOME CHEER.

TO EAT AND REST, AND WALK AND PLAY,
IS LUTHER'S FARE THROUGHOUT THE DAY,
OR RUN WITH BALL AND SNIFF THE GROUND,
OF ANY ALIEN THAT DARES TO SOUND.

POOR LUTHER'S CHIN HAS GONE QUITE GREY,
HIS YEARS THEY PASS LIKE BREAK OF DAY,
BUT AT HALF PAST TEN WITHOUT A CLOCK,
IT'S STRAIGHT TO BED, AND NONE WILL MOCK.

A COLLIE DOG, FOR MINDING SHEEP,
IS GUARDING NOW THE SHEPHERD'S SLEEP,
IN DREAMS HIS PAWS RUN, WHILE FLAT OUT,
HIS WORK IS DONE, NO NEED TO SCOUT.

TO TRUST HIS MASTER, HE KNOWS IS KIND,
OUR MASTER TOO WILL ALWAYS FIND,
FOR WHEN WE STRAY HE TAKES US HOME,
AND NOT A WORD, JUST, GLAD WELCOME.

(Manresa 1998)

THROW-AWAY DOG

WHO THREW LUTHER AWAY, ON A COLD EMPTY NIGHT,
ACROSS THE CHURCH WALL AND OUT OF SIGHT?
OR WHY DID YOU WANDER, AWAY FROM A HOME,
WERE YOU LOST, ABANDONED, LIKE A VERSELESS POEM?

INTO THE CHURCHYARD, BLOODSHOT EYES,
RIB CAGE OUT AND NO NINE LIVES,
ALTHOUGH A DOG, YOU FORAGED IN BINS,
IN THROUGH THE CHURCH YOU WERE TAKEN IN.

PAUL AND HIS DAD, AND NEIGHBOURS CARED,
BUT YOUR BOLDNESS SAT YOU IN THE CHURCH PORCH AIR,
LIKE YOU BELONGED AND WAITED TO BE FED AND LOVED,
IT'S THE LEAST YOU EXPECT FROM THE FRUITS OF THE DOVE.

A CHRISTMAS DOG DUMPED, AFTER PLAYED AS A TOY,
OR A DEAD NEIGHBOUR'S KIN, TRYING A PLOY,
YET SOMEBODY OWNED YOU AND NO LONGER CARED,
SO YOU WANDERED AND MADE A CHURCHMAN'S LAIR.

NOT IN THE YARD, THAT WON'T DO,
NOR A KENNEL OR BOX, THEY DON'T HAVE A CLUE,
BUT INTO THE HOUSE AND INTO THE CHAIR,
AND SLEEP ON THE BED, AT LAST, THIS IS CARE.

SOMETIMES WE FORGET THAT DOGS KNOW TOO,
WHERE LOVE IS FOR REAL, AND NOT A RUE,
AN ANIMAL'S LIFE IS PART OF GOD'S PLAN,
FOR ALL NATURE WAITS, THE ETERNAL SPAN.

BE IT PLANTS OR A DOG, OR A CAT OR A TREE,
WE ARE MEASURED IN TRUTH BY THE WAY WE SEE,
THAT THEY'RE PART OF OUR WORLD, OUR REACTION WILL SHOW,
HOW FAR OUR LONG PRAYERS, MIGHT HAVE FARTHER TO GO.

(Dundrum 1998)

Prospect Cottage

Dear Bernard Kennedy
Many thanks for yr
book and the seeds for next morning
next spring. Strange I was
thinking should I plant —
wallflower seeds or buy plants
in the autumn. The seeds
are going in — I'll settle
down with the poems later as
we are putting down a floor
and there is much banging
going on — working on film
of Ludwig Wittgenstein who
visited Ireland at the end of
his life with Tariq Ali ('60'
revolutionary) as producer he's
charming and great fun
       regards & thanks Derek

PLANTS FOR THE AUTUMN[33]
(For derek jarman)

AUTUMN IS THE TIME,
AS SPRING IS, AND SUMMER,
A TIME FOR CHRONOS.

TIME FOR LEAVES TO FALL,
FROM A BOOK OF LIFE.

A LIFE OF DEREK JARMAN.
TOO COLOURFUL FOR AUTUMN,
BUT BEFORE SPRING,
YOU DIED.
YOUR PASTELS WERE READY
AS FILM JOURNEY OF
HINT, SUGGESTION AND SHOUT.

AN AVANT GARDE LIFE OF
COLOUR, ALWAYS SPRING,
JUST ONE AUTUMN FALL.
COLOURFUL, THOUGH YOU DIED,
IN A BLACK AND WHITE MONTH,
IN A BLACK AND WHITE ISSUE,
FOR SOME.

PLANTS FOR THE AUTUMN,
FEBRUARY SNOW CAME, WHITE
OF THE BLACK.
THOUGH STATED COLOUR
OF SUMMER'S BLAZE.

(Dundrum 1998)

Index of First Lines

A fetid, putrid, rotten, evil smell,	71
After the storm comes the silence of hush,	113
A lyrical muezzin	99
Alone in the darkness of your inner feel,	114
And time moves on,	111
Another rained-out fortnight,	83
A scene without carpets,	81
A small seed is a child	23
As you lie there, flat as a pancake,	74
At the darkest, deadest, depressed	31
A tunnel feel comes down to us,	45
Autumn is a time,	121
Between its teeth, the wicked cat,	63
Come close dear Mars,	51
Cracking rock of burning coal,	7
Cut-back among leaves of autumn,	107
Eastward slave,	5
From my priest's window	86
Gabriel comes and Raphael too,	14
Going home fast, the kids	97
Have I grown onwards so fast,	21
Have you ever thought	43
Heel heel, and constant peal	3
He is a T.V. personality,	37
He was hungry for dinner at eight,	59
Hind legs, swift push, forward,	35
How do you stand so erect,	65
I love to hear the silence of the night,	16
I met my father,	9
I love to hear the silence of the night,	16
In the distance over the tops of roofs,	15
In the evening corner,	41
I saw a rook rush downwards	13
I sometimes see you on a bicycle,	38
I think I like the evening best of all,	25
I travelled like a Sultan,	69

I walked in my bare feet bare, on the grass	93
Laughter is red and rosy,	57
Like a ghostly shroud,	89
Lying prostrate on a marble slab	36
Mother, our human gods relative,	30
Minarets and mosques,	67
Mise Éire	95
Now September comes and school begins	27
Now school begins again	29
Over twenty-three years ago and since,	11
Poor Father Shawn, for many years,	115
Sail on past,	53
Sometimes we hear the boat man's call,	47
Svelte love, with your amorous charms,	73
Tall and black ladies of prayer,	39
Temple Bar, Latin Quarter, Left Bank,	79
That naked, nuanced, emptied talk is soundless.	108
The fields are on fire,	105
The giant great gentle oak is there and stays,	109
The market place	112
The necklace in the link continues	101
The priest just rang to say,	18
There is a line,	4
There's only a baby in the manger,	33
These are the days that I will cherish,	55
The silent night makes loud the hissing log,	32
Troubled souls with disjointed life,	26
Walking by as children,	61
"What a view from up here.	92
Who threw Luther away, on a cold empty night,	119
Who's this curled at my heel in bed?	118
With a donor kebab,	91
Would Shelley or Byron	103

Notes on the poems

[1] Marlay: a former demesne, now a public park, in south Dublin.

[2] Northern man: develops an idea that personality and mores are connected.

[3] Celts are possibly from Galatia, or Anatolian Plateau, prior to becoming a nomadic people, then settling in Ireland.

[4] An excavation suggested Midas was a real king.

[5] Kilmashogue: part of the Wicklow Way, leading from Marlay.

[6] A retreat house of prayer, run by the Jesuit Fathers in Clontarf, Dublin.

[7] From Manresa grounds can be heard one of the bells of the Clontarf churches.

[8] Playing on the theme night/dark, and redemption, beginning in the darkness.

[9] St Enda's Park or Coláiste Eanna: a private school run by Padraic Pearse, Irish patriot and embryo of the Irish Rebellion of 1916.

[10] Balbriggan: a north county Dublin seaside town.

[11] Written to commemorate grotto in Loreto grounds, Balbriggan.

[12] A new style crib, with only the child, erected in St. Philomena's Church, Palmerstown, 1993. Removed because too modern.

[13] Luther: author's pet, border collie, saved from the street, 1994.

[14] Names varieties of roses in garden, at Palmerstown, now at Sweetmount, Dundrum.

[15] Thetis: one of the Nereid, daughter of old man of the sea, Nereus and Doris. Mother of Achilles. Achilles: featured in homer and Euripides, fought at Troy, was almost destroyed when Apollo guided an arrow to his only weak spot, his heel. He knew not fear. Adonis: from Syrian legend, a river, the Adonis flows near Byblos. Aphrodite's tears created roses and Adonis's anemones. Styx river of the underworld. The eldest of Oceanus children. Thetis dipped Achilles heel in this river, to make him invulnerable. Virgil places Styx as a river around Hades.

[16] Marmara Sea: surrounds the Golden Horn at Istanbul.

[17] Dolmabache: in Istanbul, last sultans residence, now museum to Ataturk, (the Turk)

[18] Kemal Mustafa Ataturk: rescued the Ottoman Empire from ruin, created the modern state Turkey, first democrat and leader, modernising the area.

[19] Chai (tea) Aryan (yoghurt) Aziyade, lover of Pierre Loti. A French Turkophile (Julien Vieaud).

[20] Xeniphon: led Roman campaign throughout the Ottoman Empire, victorious at modern Trabzon where, weary from war, the soldiers rejoiced seeing ships.

[21] People wonder who the dark lady in Shakespearean sonnets was.

[22] Barbara Frietchie: A poem by American poet John Greenleaf Whittier (1807 to 1892) known by heart by subject in her 'four score and ten'.

[23] Ortakoy: fashionable place by the sea, in Istanbul.

[24] Yeni Kapi: a bay walk at Istanbul, with city view.

[25] Ani: ancient city on Turkish-Russian Border.

[26] Trabzon: coastal Black Sea towards north-eastern Turkey.

[27] In 1520, Inigo of Loyola spent time in a cave in Manresa, North Spain, which prompted change from soldier to saint.

[28] St. Paul in his second letter to Corinth Ch.15 v. 55 asks "Death where is your sting".

[29] In Book of Genesis Ch. 23, Jacob wrestles with an angel.

[30] Refers to Paul "Thorn in the flesh" mentioned in the 2nd letter to Corinth Ch. 12 v. 7/8.

[31] Refers to the story of Emmaus in Luke's Gospel Ch. 24 v. 13/35.

[32] Rublev's Icon of Trinity, leaves space at front for the viewer.

[33] Based on letter to author, from jarman, deciding to put in his garden 'plants for autumn'. derek jarman: writer and film producer, died February 1994.